HYPERDOCUMENTS

and How to Create Them

A  **BOOK**

THE JAMES MARTIN BOOKS
currently available from Prentice Hall

- Application Development Without Programmers
- Building Expert Systems
- Communications Satellite Systems
- Computer Data-Base Organization, Second Edition
- The Computerized Society
- Computer Networks and Distributed Processing: Software, Techniques, and Architecture
- Data Communication Technology
- DB2: Concepts, Design, and Programming
- Design and Strategy of Distributed Data Processing
- Design of Real-Time Computer Systems
- An End User's Guide to Data Base
- Fourth-Generation Languages, Volume I: Principles
- Fourth-Generation Languages, Volume II: Representative 4GLs
- Fourth-Generation Languages, Volume III: 4GLs from IBM
- Future Developments in Telecommunications, Second Edition
- Hyperdocuments and How to Create Them
- IBM Office Systems: Architectures and Implementations
- IDMS/R: Concepts, Design, and Programming
- Information Engineering, Book I: Introduction and Principles
- Information Engineering, Book II: Planning and Analysis
- Information Engineering, Book III: Design and Construction
- An Information Systems Manifesto
- Local Area Networks: Architectures and Implementations
- Managing the Data-Base Environment
- Principles of Data-Base Management
- Principles of Data Communication
- Recommended Diagramming Standards for Analysts and Programmers
- SNA: IBM's Networking Solution
- Strategic Information Planning Methodologies, Second Edition
- System Design from Provably Correct Constructs
- Systems Analysis for Data Transmission
- Technology's Crucible
- Telecommunications and the Computer, Third Edition
- Telematic Society: A Challenge for Tomorrow
- VSAM: Access Method Services and Programming Techniques

with Carma McClure

- Action Diagrams: Clearly Structured Specifications, Programs, and Procedures, Second Edition
- Diagramming Techniques for Analysts and Programmers
- Software Maintenance: The Problem and Its Solutions
- Structured Techniques: The Basis for CASE, Revised Edition

HYPERDOCUMENTS
and How to Create Them

JAMES MARTIN

PRENTICE HALL, Englewood Cliffs, New Jersey 07632

Library of Congress Cataloging-in-Publication Data

Martin, James (date)
    Hyperdocuments & how to create them / James Martin.
      p. cm.
    "The James Martin books."
    Includes bibliographical references.
    ISBN 0-13-447905-X
    1. Hypertext systems. I. Title. II. Title: Hyperdocuments and
how to create them.
  QA76.76.H94M27 1990   89-70991
  005.75—dc20   CIP

Editorial/production supervision: *Kathryn Gollin Marshak*
Cover design: *Wanda Lubelska Design*
Manufacturing buyer: *Ray Sintel*

Copyright © 1990 by James Martin

 Published by Prentice-Hall, Inc.
A division of Simon & Schuster
Englewood Cliffs, New Jersey 07632

The publisher offers discounts on this book when ordered
in bulk quantities. For more information write or call:
      Special Sales; Prentice-Hall, Inc.
      College Technical and Reference Division
      Englewood Cliffs, NJ 07632
      (201)592-2498

Printed in the United States of America

10 9 8 7 6 5 4 3 2

ISBN   0-13-447905-X

PRENTICE-HALL INTERNATIONAL (UK) LIMITED, *London*
PRENTICE-HALL OF AUSTRALIA PTY. LIMITED, *Sydney*
PRENTICE-HALL CANADA INC., *Toronto*
PRENTICE-HALL HISPANOAMERICANA, S.A., *Mexico*
PRENTICE-HALL OF INDIA PRIVATE LIMITED, *New Delhi*
PRENTICE-HALL OF JAPAN, INC., *Tokyo*
SIMON & SCHUSTER ASIA PTE. LTD., *Singapore*
EDITORA PRENTICE-HALL DO BRASIL, LTDA., *Rio De Janeiro*

TO CORINTHIA

CONTENTS

PART **II**   # HOW TO ORGANIZE HYPERDOCUMENTS

7 Documents with Embedded Intelligence 73

8 Helping the User Navigate 81

PART III GUIDELINES FOR AUTHORS

9 The Process of Hyperdocument Creation 95

PREFACE

As software, procedures, and systems become ever more complex, paper documentation becomes ever more bulky. Massive amounts of paper are difficult to use and expensive to update. Fortunately, we have entered the era of electronic documentation. Electronic documents can be physically small (for example, CD-ROMs), can be easy to navigate through, can be searched at high speed, can help their users with built-in training or expert systems, and can be updated electronically.

The term *hyperdocument* refers to an electronic document which combines hypertext with diagrams, possibly sound, animation, or video, and possibly other types of software, such as spreadsheets, computer-based training, decision-support software, rule-based processing, or expert systems. With hyperdocument software we can create "intelligent documents" which guide their users, have built-in artificial intelligence or expertise, and can adapt themselves to users' needs. Many separate documents can be electronically interlinked. As rapidly as possible, we want the massive documentation of industry and government to become "intelligent."

Hyperdocuments deliver information in ways that go beyond paperwork and database methods. Their information is extensively cross-referenced, with fact linked to fact linked to fact. They should be designed to help solve their users' problems, employing whatever graphics, audio-video, or other digital media are appropriate, linked to whatever software can make the information more useful.

Paperwork regulation, manuals, and libraries are often so bulky and complex that civil servants, lawyers, product users, and others spend much time searching for information but often fail to find items that are important to them. Good hyperdocuments help solve this problem. The CALS (Computer-Aided Acquisition and Logistics Support) initiative of the U.S. Department of Defense alone represents a billion-dollar market for hyperdocuments. All computer and software manuals should be delivered electronically. Police files with information about large numbers of crimes, criminals, and suspects should be electronically interlinked to help detectives search for potential criminals with a modus operandi or other clues that may help solve a crime. In the future most professionals will use vast amounts of knowledge stored on optical discs in hyperdocument form.

A danger with hyperdocuments has been well demonstrated in the early *hypertext* systems (which used electronically interlinked text). It is easy for the creator of a hyperdocument to create a mass of linkages which confuse the reader. The user becomes lost in spaghetti. When society acquires new media, it is necessary for a sense of style to evolve about how to use the media as effectively as possible. Hyperdocuments are a very important and complex new medium. It is easy to create bad hyperdocuments—hyper*chaos*.

This book explains the technology of hyperdocuments and describes applications of the technology. It attempts, to describe what is good and bad in the creation of hyperdocuments and, hence, act as a *style guide* for authors working with this exciting new medium.

The advice in the book is based on experience in creating a number of diverse hyperdocuments, including methodologies for software development, a complex model of future technology, software surveys, and an "encyclopedia" of human factoring. It is clear that authoring techniques that work well with hyperdocuments are different from those that work well with books. Many of the techniques of seminar presentation are appropriate to the creation of hyperdocuments.

Much "reverse engineering" is needed to put today's paperwork into electronic form (for example, auditors' regulations, documentation for maintaining machines, software manuals, architects' catalogues and drawings). Chapter 16 discusses this conversion process. Although paper documents can be converted directly to electronic form, most need to be restructured and partially reauthored to take advantage of the medium.

To create good hyperdocuments requires clear thinking about the subject matter, the presentation techniques, and the users' needs. Hyperdocument software can be a great help in the thinking process. Indeed, an author of a textbook or report, or a person preparing a seminar or video production, can benefit greatly from hyperdocument authoring software because it helps organize random thoughts into the most effective structures. Reports or textbooks written as hyperdocuments usually turn out to be better on paper because their ideas are better organized.

The best hyperdocuments "feel" much smaller than they are. Using a mouse, the user can navigate through the document very rapidly. Although the document may contain a vast amount of information, the user can quickly find the nuggets of information which can help him.

It is hoped that authors of hypertext or hyperdocuments will study this short book and that it will help them create better products.

James Martin

HYPERDOCUMENTS

and How to Create Them

PART **I** **INTRODUCTION**

1 WHAT ARE HYPERMEDIA?

Fundamental changes have occurred in civilization when humankind has learned to communicate in new ways. When humans first developed speech they became different from the animals, because ideas and information could be exchanged and improved upon. When humankind learned to write, ideas could be stored and preserved for posterity. After the invention of the printing press, ideas and information could be circulated among many people. Broadcasting enabled news and ideas to reach vast numbers of people simultaneously.

Books, broadcasting, newsprint, and television are one-way media. The user takes what is fed to him*. The computer provides a fundamentally different medium. The user interacts with it. The computer employs logic to help its user. It can employ stored expertise. It can adapt its presentation of information to the immediate needs of the user. The computer is active, whereas books, print and television are passive.

The computer has another fundamental difference: it can provide access to vast amounts of information. A single 4¾-inch CD-ROM (compact disk read-only memory) can store a quite overwhelming amount of text—270,000 pages—and computers can access huge libraries of information on other media. This ocean of data can be reproduced endlessly and made accessible with telecommunications.

COMPUTER-AIDED NAVIGATION *Hypermedia* employ information under the control of a computer so that the user of the information can navigate through it in valuable ways. The information may be in the form of text, diagrams, moving diagrams (animation), images, moving images (television), speech, sound, or computer programs.

---

*: "He" and "him" are used to mean either gender throughout the book.

To navigate through hypermedia, the user employs "buttons" that are made visible in some way on the screen of a computer or television set. The user activates the button and the computer responds. It may display different text; it may display a diagram, an image, or a note in a window; it may generate speech or other sound; it may display moving video.

The user can easily reverse the action of the button to return to the screen situation that existed before the button was activated.

HYPERTEXT AND HYPERDOCS

A common form of hypermedia is hypertext in which information is in the form of text displayed on a computer screen. Unlike text in a book the reader can traverse computerized links to skip almost instantly to other parts of the text. The text is threaded with links designed so that the reader can flash from one place to another in useful ways.

Computers are good at displaying diagrams and images. Diagrams are extremely valuable in explaining complex concepts. The key to writing technical textbooks is to devise diagrams that are as communicative as possible. Diagrams are even more important in communicating via hypermedia. We will use the term *hyperdocument,* rather than *hypertext,* to refer to a computerized document that has diagrams and, possibly, images, sound, animation, video, and computer programs as well as text.

Sometimes the abbreviated form of the word is used: *hyperdoc.*

Most hyperdocuments are designed for use with a personal computer. They can be explored using the keyboard and possibly a mouse. The user can open and close layers of the document at high speed, can display windows, flip rapidly through pages, perform computer-speed searches, scroll different windows, display buttons of different types, and follow hyperlinks to jump through the document in diverse ways, exploring what is useful to him. The user may be able to leave the electronic bookmarks or notes in the document and indicate what parts of the document are valuable or valueless to him.

To appreciate the value of hyperdocuments, it is necessary to use them for a while, getting a feel for their power and elegance. It is difficult to appreciate this by reading about them, just as it is difficult to obtain feel for the power of spreadsheet tools without using them.

The most revolutionary change in computing in the 1980s was the spread of computers on the desktop; the most revolutionary change in the 1990s will be the spread of vast libraries of information to the desktop. The challenge is to make this deluge of information as valuable as possible to the user (Fig. 1.1).

HYPERLINKS

The information in hypermedia is threaded with links so that the user can traverse almost immediately from one part of the information to another. The reader does not progress through a

```
T *              24.95        ᴌ
* *               1.81     TX ×
D  694           26.76     TL *


D  694           26.76   MSC
                         TND
D  694            0.00   CNG


0 0 0 0 0 1 / 0 9 / 9 0
```

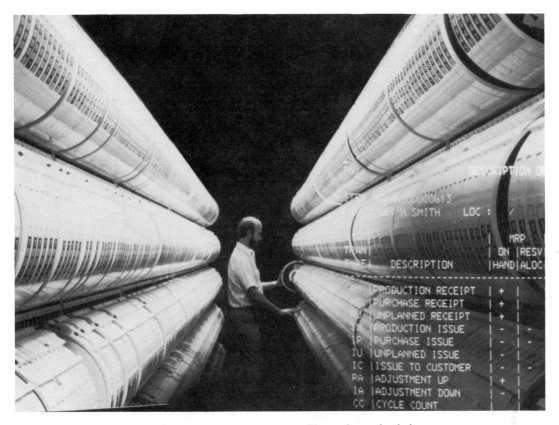

Figure 1.1 As much data as exists in this room will soon be on the desktop.
(Photo courtesy of National Center for Atmospheric Research/National Science Foundation.)

document sequentially but makes electronic leaps from one part to another (Fig. 1.2).

The link is often referred to as a *hyperlink* to make clear its function. The term *hyperlink* is also used as a verb; we say one part of a document is hyperlinked to another. At the start of the hyperlink is a *button* which the reader may activate if he wishes. At the end of the hyperlink is a *target* (Fig. 1.3).

BUTTONS   A button is usually one of the following:

- A word in text
- A contiguous group of words in text
- A marked area of a diagram
- A label on part of a diagram

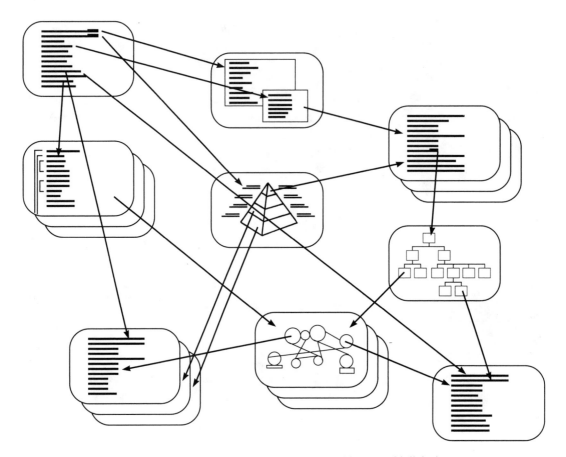

Figure 1.2 Hyperdocuments contain text and images with links interconnecting them so that a reader can skip almost instantly from one piece of information to another.

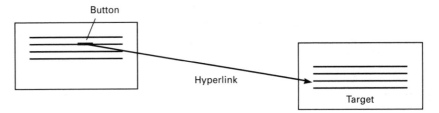

Figure 1.3 Different parts of documents are connected by hyperlinks which the reader can follow almost instantaneously. At the start of the hyperlink is a button which the reader can activate if he wishes; at the end is a target. The target may be in the same document as the button or may be in a different document.

The button is made visible by reverse video, color, or use of a pop-on box on a diagram. The user may point to the button with a mouse or may highlight the button by using keys.

TARGETS

The target to which a link connects could be one of several types of item:

- A line of text
- A segment of a hyperdocument containing an idea or concept
- Another document
- A picture
- A moving video or animation sequence
- A program

When the button is activated it results in one or more of the following:

- **Open/close.** A document or segment of a document may be opened so that the user can read it or closed so that it becomes an icon or title line.
- **Expand/contract.** An item on the screen may be expanded into more detail or contracted to one line. With multiple CONTRACT actions, the user can see a summary of the document structure.
- **Jump.** A different part of the document is displayed.
- **Display a definition.** A glossary definition is displayed in a window.
- **Display a tutorial.** A tutorial explanation of the button word(s) is displayed. The tutorial itself may be a small document.
- **Display a note.** A note is displayed in a window.
- **Display a diagram.** A diagram is displayed relating to the button word(s).
- **Display a moving diagram.** An animated picture is displayed.
- **Play a sound sequence.** Recorded sound is played, for example, spoken explanation of a chart.
- **Display a video sequence.** A television sequence may be displayed on the whole computer screen, in a window, or on a separate screen.
- **Execute a program.** A program is initiated, for example, an expert system, a spreadsheet tool, or a program to which the hyperdocument is subordinate.

Whenever a button is activated, it is desirable that the reverse action can be taken quickly to return the user to the situation prior to his pressing the button.

THREADS A *thread* is a collection of links which the user can follow contiguously. He may do this by repeatedly pressing one key. The thread strings together ideas, images, or modules of a hyperdocument which may be usefully examined in sequence.

WINDOWS Some hyperdocuments employ windows. A user may have multiple windows on his computer screen simultaneously. It is particularly important for the author of a hyperdocument to have two scrollable windows so that he can see the button which he builds and the target at the same time.

ACCESS TO A CENTRAL REPOSITORY Multiple hyperdocuments may link to a central repository which contains material such as the following:

- Glossary
- List of acronym definitions
- Collection of diagrams
- Collection of tutorial modules relating to the concepts in the documents
- Collection of references
- Collection of general information such as vendors, addresses, people to contact

The buttons and hyperlinks to the glossary, acronym list, or tutorial modules should be built *automatically* by the software.

Many computer systems store vast amounts of information. The challenge of computing today is to help the user employ this information to solve problems.

2 WHY HYPERDOCUMENTS?

Hyperdocuments are never likely to replace all books and reports. The completely paperless society will probably never arrive. Paper has attractive qualities as a delivery medium. You can take books to bed and read them on the bus. You can scan large areas of print in a newspaper.

When book-sized display screens improve, it may become attractive to read electronic books in bed. Small optical storage devices will eventually make digital information cheaper than paperbacks. If such a device contained a novel in text, it would present information in a similar way to a book. The reader would start at the front and progress sequentially, occasionally skipping, looking at a table of contents, and, maybe, stealing a glance at the end. Most other documents will not be read sequentially. The reader will expand and contract the document structure as fast as he can flip through book pages. He will zip over hyperlinks, trying to learn and find information more rapidly than he can with a book. He can traverse the information instantly, hyperlinking in and out of diagrams. The information becomes fluid.

Electronic documents should not be imitations of paper documents. They bring major new types of benefits. The first cars were called "horseless carriages" and looked as though they were designed to be pulled by a horse. It took many years to realize that a good shape for a car is quite different. Radio was originally called "wireless telegraphy"; it took years to realize that the great application of radio was broadcasting, which had no resemblance to telegraphy. Similarly, "paperless books" should have little resemblance to books in the way they are designed.

We must ask: What benefits can electronic documents have that paper documents do not have?

THE COST ADVANTAGE

Optical disks have brought us to an important milestone in human history. The cost of digital storage is much cheaper than the cost of paper. Today this cost difference is realizable only with large documents. A vast amount of information can be stored on a 4¾ -inch optical disk. A CD-ROM can hold the equivalent of hundreds of books and be mass-produced for the price of one book (the price of a music CD).

It is economic, and highly desirable, to put bulky manuals on optical storage. As small computers proliferate and storage devices drop in cost, it becomes economic to put less bulky and less expensive documentation into computers. The cost of electronic media will continue to drop rapidly until many people have "microbooks," perhaps with optical disks 2 inches or less in diameter.

BULKY DOCUMENTS

The world is full of bulky manuals for equipment of many types, government regulations, auditors' and accountants' procedures, detailed methodologies, and so on. It is desirable to put lawyers' libraries, medical knowledge, United Nations data books and market research documents on CD-ROMs. The manuals of all computer software ought be on its users' computers in hyperdocument form.

It is said that, for every four Chrysler M1 tanks that go into battle, an armored personnel carrier must accompany them carrying the documentation needed for their maintenance. The documentation for a jet fighter weighs more than the plane. If stacked in one pile, the documentation for a North Sea oil rig would be higher than the oil rig.

One CD-ROM contains the equivalent of about an 80-foot-high stack of text reports on paper. The writeable optical WORM (write-once read-many times) disk for personal computers contains somewhat more than this—800 megabytes. (See Fig. 2.1.)

In the early nineteenth century, the world's information doubled every half century. Now it doubles every three years. The doubling time continues to shrink rapidly (Fig. 2.2). With the advent of optical disks and computer networks, a good part of this mass of data is potentially available to our desk computer. We will desperately need ways to navigate through this deluge of data so that it can be made as useful as possible.

MAINTENANCE PROBLEMS

Many paper manuals, technical reports, product reviews, and so on are updated frequently. Paper updates are sent out which the recipient is supposed to insert into the appropriate place in the document binders. Often the updates are never inserted. This maintenance problem is avoided if the documentation is on CD-ROM and a current version of the disk is sent out periodically.

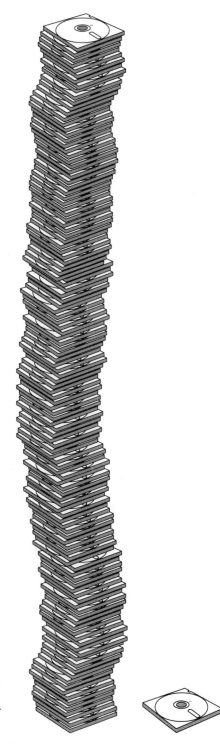

Figure 2.1 One optical WORM disk contains
800 megabytes—the equivalent of 2222 × 360-
kilobyte floppy disks or about a hundred feet of
bookshelves.

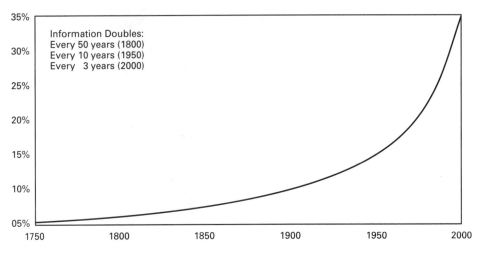

Figure 2.2 Annual percentage increase in world's information. (From 1987 Pacific Telesis Annual Report.)

If the material is in hyperdocument form, it should be designed so that, when changes are made, a computer automatically rebuilds the hyperlinks. A spaghettilike mess of hyperlinks with no automated maintenance can render hyperdocuments useless. Well-designed electronic documents, however, have much lower maintenance costs than does paper documentation.

WHAT CAN BE DONE ELECTRONICALLY THAT CANNOT BE DONE ON PAPER

Often, the true value of hyperdocuments lies not in lower costs but in the user being able to learn faster, find information faster, or put stored knowledge to use more effectively. There are many advantages which hyperdocuments have which paper alone does not have. These are listed in Fig. 2.3 and expanded upon in Fig. 2.4. If this were a hyperdocument, we could select any of the items in Fig. 2.3 and expand it, as shown in Fig. 2.4.

URGENTLY NEEDED HYPERDOCUMENTS

Perhaps the most urgent need for hyperdocuments is to replace paper documentation for complex products and procedures. Computer operating systems and software become ever more complex and their documentation ever more voluminous. Such documentation is cumbersome, difficult to update, and difficult to use. It clearly ought to be delivered in electronic form. Putting bulky documents on a CD-ROM makes them easy to distribute and update, but does not, by itself, make them easy to use.

Benefits of Hyperdocuments That Paper Documents Do Not Have

... The reader can follow hyperlinks at high speed.
... The document can have complex and interesting structures.
... The document can have intelligence built into it.
... The document may include sound, animation, or video.
... Reusable nuggets of information can be used in many places.
... Documents can include computer-based training.
... The document can adapt itself to the reader.
... The reader can mark the document in interesting ways.
... Much more complete indexing is feasible than with paper.
... Brute-force searching can be used.
... Documents of vast size can be used.
... Documents can be designed for ease of updating.
... Many documents can be linked.
... Documents can be dynamic and constantly updated.
... Portions of documents can be hidden for security reasons.
... Portions of documents can be hidden to avoid bewildering the reader.
... The document may be a part of other software.

Figure 2.3   Benefits of hyperdocuments that paper documents do not have.
Any line on this document can be *expanded*. See Fig 2.4.

Ease of use requires a document navigation procedure which relates to the user's needs. Paper documents provide a table of contents and an index. Hyperdocuments can provide far more useful ways to navigate through complex or bulky information. The user of a hyperdocument should be able to find what he needs more quickly and with greater certainty than when confronted with massive paper manuals. To achieve this important goal, the hyperdocument must be well designed. The user of a poorly designed electronic document will react negatively to it, be bewildered by it, and often fail to find what he needs.

DOCUMENTS WITH BUILT-IN EXPERTISE

Hyperdocuments can have intelligence built into them in the way an expert system has. Solutions can be hyperlinked to user problems or issues. The user may need to take actions such as deciding what product to buy, determining how to fix a broken machine or how to use software correctly. The hyperdocument can contain built-in expertise to guide the user. It may provide action-oriented solutions to problems or issues.

When the user first opens the hyperdocument on the screen, he does not know how it is structured. The software should make its structure visible to the user and guide the user so that he finds the information that is most valuable to him.

Benefits of hyperdocuments that paper documents do not have

The reader can follow hyperlinks at high speed
He can link:
- to more detailed explanations
- to pictures
- from parts of pictures to explanatory text
- to reference information
- to a glossary

The documents can have complex and interesting structures.
The document could be structured around diagrams, the reader having the ability to link from the diagram structure to the text.
The reader can navigate logically (as opposed to physically) around the document, at high speed.
The reader can very rapidly expand and contract areas of the document.

The document can have intelligence built into it.
When a hyperlink is followed:
- rule-based processing may occur
- computations may be performed
- the document may ask the user questions
The document may have an expert system built into it, for example a maintenance manual may give help in diagnosing machine problems.
The document may help to solve user problems, for example by relating issues to their possible solutions.

The document may include sound, animation, or video.
A conventional computer may produce sound and animation.
A multimedia computer may contain segments of video, digitized and compressed (e.g., with a DVI board for display).
The computer may be linked to a CD-I unit for high-quality music, speech, and graphics.
The computer may be linked to a laserdisk system so that selected segments of video may be displayed.

Reusable nuggets of information can be used in many places.
There may be an author's index of reusable nuggets of information.
Multiple documents may share an index of reusable nuggets of information.

Documents can include computer-based training.

The document can adapt itself to the reader.
The document can indicate what the reader has already looked at.
The computer can know the reader's skills.
The reader can mark whether he likes what he has read.
The document can adapt itself to the likes and skills of the reader.

The reader can mark the document in interesting ways.
The reader can use electronic bookmarks.
The reader can indicate what parts of the document he might want to revisit.
The reader can effectively delete what he does not find useful in order to simplify his view of the document.
The deleted part is hidden but not lost.
The reader can leave annotations anywhere in the document, which will be displayed in windows.

Much more complete indexing is feasible than with paper.

Brute-force searching can be used.
The computer can find every occurrence of a search word or phrase, possibly skipping at the user's request from one occurrence to the next.
The computer can replace every occurrence of a word with a different word.

Figure 2.4 Expansion of Figure 2.3.

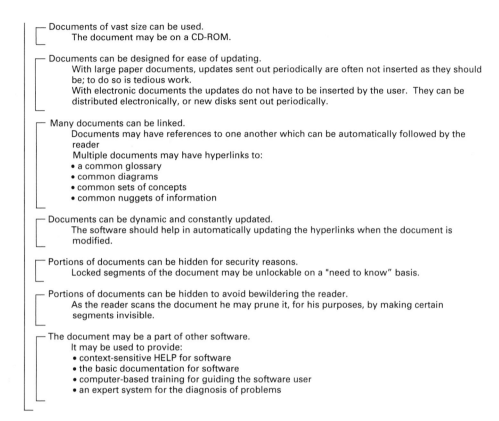

Documents of vast size can be used.
  The document may be on a CD-ROM.

Documents can be designed for ease of updating.
  With large paper documents, updates sent out periodically are often not inserted as they should
  be; to do so is tedious work.
  With electronic documents the updates do not have to be inserted by the user. They can be
  distributed electronically, or new disks sent out periodically.

Many documents can be linked.
  Documents may have references to one another which can be automatically followed by the
  reader
  Multiple documents may have hyperlinks to:
  • a common glossary
  • common diagrams
  • common sets of concepts
  • common nuggets of information

Documents can be dynamic and constantly updated.
  The software should help in automatically updating the hyperlinks when the document is
  modified.

Portions of documents can be hidden for security reasons.
  Locked segments of the document may be unlockable on a "need to know" basis.

Portions of documents can be hidden to avoid bewildering the reader.
  As the reader scans the document he may prune it, for his purposes, by making certain
  segments invisible.

The document may be a part of other software.
  It may be used to provide:
  • context-sensitive HELP for software
  • the basic documentation for software
  • computer-based training for guiding the software user
  • an expert system for the diagnosis of problems

Figure 2.4   (Continued)

HYPERDOCUMENTS FOR DIAGNOSIS AND REPAIR

Figure 2.5 shows an overview structure of a document designed to help in diagnosing and correcting problems. The user problems are the blocks at the top of the diagram. Each user problem has underneath it a number of possible failure modes that could be the cause of the problem. Each failure mode is itself subdivided into lower-level failure modes. There is a hierarchy of failure modes for each user problem. Some failure modes for one problem may be the same as for another problem. For each failure mode, there may be one or more tests which can be used to confirm whether that type of failure is occurring. When a type of failure is confirmed, the document may state in detail what repair action should be taken.

Figure 2.6 presents the same information as in Fig. 2.5 drawn with a hierarchy of brackets. This is generally a useful way to represent compound documents because the user can open and close brackets and scroll up and down the text very rapidly.

Figure 2.7 gives a specific illustration of a document designed for diagno-

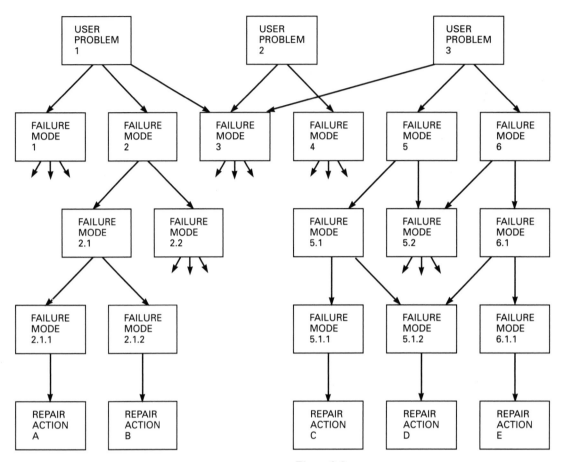

Figure 2.5

sis. The overall problem addressed in Fig. 2.7 is that a motorbike will not start. The diagram gives a hierarchy of possible reasons. Any of the FAILURE MODE lines may be expanded into more detailed text. The text may state tests that can be performed to determine the causes of failure and repair actions that can be taken to correct the problem.

The FAILURE MODE "dead battery," for example, is expanded into more detail in Fig. 2.8. The detail shows two tests, results of which confirm or disconfirm that the battery is dead and actions which should be taken. The descriptions of tests and actions may be of any length; they may themselves be hyperdocuments with a useful structure, containing text, pictures, possibly speech or video, buttons, and hyperlinks.

The illustration in Figs. 2.7 and 2.8 is simple. The reader should extend the ideas in his imagination to elaborate systems with massive documentation, which require considerable diagnosis expertise.

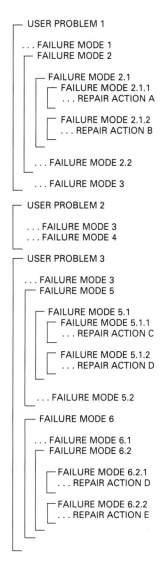

Figure 2.6 Envelope diagram showing the structure drawn in Figure 2.5. Any of the lines preceded by dots can be expanded into more detail. The detail may include text, pictures, speech, or video segments, all connected by buttons and hyperlinks.

USER GUIDANCE   Hyperdocuments for diagnosis, as illustrated in Fig. 2.6, are one form of document designed to guide its user to solve problems. There are many other forms of hyperdocument which actively help the user. The document should be designed with the users' needs in mind.

Hyperdocuments may be designed to help the user employ complex software. When the user presses the HELP key, an appropriate part of the hyperdocument may be displayed to explain what he needs to know. Software documentation should generally be in hyperdocument form, and context-oriented

```
┌─ USER PROBLEM: Motorbike will not start.

  . . . FAILURE MODE 1: Engine starts and stalls.
  ┌─ FAILURE MODE 2: Engine fails to start.

     ┌─ FAILURE MODE 2.1: No spark at spark plug.

        . . . FAILURE MODE 2.1.1: Dead battery.
        . . . FAILURE MODE 2.1.2: Discharged battery.
        . . . FAILURE MODE 2.1.3: Spark plug problems.
        . . . FAILURE MODE 2.1.4: Charging system problems.

     ┌─ FAILURE MODE 2.2: Has spark at spark plug.

        . . . FAILURE MODE 2.2.1: Clogged fuel lines.
        . . . FAILURE MODE 2.2.2: Engine oil too heavy.
        . . . FAILURE MODE 2.2.3: Incorrect ignition timing.
        . . . FAILURE MODE 2.2.4: Low compression.
        . . . FAILURE MODE 2.2.5: Defective breaker points.
        . . . FAILURE MODE 2.2.6: Carburetor problems.
        . . . FAILURE MODE 2.2.7: Engine seized.
```

Figure 2.7   A diagnosis and repair hyperdocument like that shown in Figure 2.6. Any of the lines preceded by dots can be expanded into more detail. The detail may include text, pictures, speech, or video segments, all connected by buttons and hyperlinks. Figure 2.8 expands the failure mode "dead battery."

```
┌─ USER PROBLEM: Motorbike will not start.

  . . . FAILURE MODE 1: Engine starts and stalls.
  ┌─ FAILURE MODE 2: Engine fails to start.

     ┌─ FAILURE MODE 2.1: No spark at spark plug.

        ┌─ FAILURE MODE 2.1.1: Dead battery.
          ┌─ TEST A: Check whether horn works; check whether lights work.
             CONFIRMING RESULT: Neither horn nor lights work.
             ACTION: Replace battery.

          ┌─ TEST B: Check battery charge.
             CONFIRMING RESULT: Less than 1.11 for one or more cells.
             DISCONFIRMING RESULT: All cells greater than 1.20.
             ACTION: Replace battery.

        . . . FAILURE MODE 2.1.2: Discharged battery.
        . . . FAILURE MODE 2.1.3: Spark plug problems.
        . . . FAILURE MODE 2.1.4: Charging system problems.

     ┌─ FAILURE MODE 2.2: Has spark at spark plug.

        . . . FAILURE MODE 2.2.1: Clogged fuel lines.
        . . . FAILURE MODE 2.2.2: Engine oil too heavy.
        . . . FAILURE MODE 2.2.3: Incorrect ignition timing.
        . . . FAILURE MODE 2.2.4: Low compression.
        . . . FAILURE MODE 2.2.5: Defective breaker points.
        . . . FAILURE MODE 2.2.6: Carburetor problems.
        . . . FAILURE MODE 2.2.7: Engine seized.
```

Figure 2.8   Envelope diagram of Figure 2.7 with expansion of failure mode "dead battery."

HELP should link into the hyperdocument at the appropriate place. Hyperdocuments can display screens from other software and place buttons on them so that the viewer can hyperlink to tutorial explanations.

Computer-based training can form a front end to an educational hyperdocument. Professionals using hyperdocuments for their own education may already know much of what is in a document, so rather than using computer-based training, they need to be able to navigate as rapidly as possible to information which is new to them.

Professionals may need education or information immediately prior to carrying out a task. They need *just-in-time* education. Often, professionals need only a small fragment of the information in a large hyperdocument. They should be able to locate what they need as rapidly as possible.

ACTIVE HYPERLINKS

The links in many hyperdocuments are GO-TO links which connect to another part of the document, link to a different document, or display a note, diagram, or window. Other types of documents can use "active" hyperlinks which perform a computation of some type.

Active hyperlinks

- Can ask a user for information.
- May perform a calculation.
- May carry out rule-based processing.
- May link to a different target on the basis of the computation.

A hyperdocument with active links may carry out a dialog with its user, possibly collecting information or determining his needs in more detail. It may modify its behavior based on its perception of its user's needs. An active hyperdocument may apply artificial intelligence techniques to make it behave in useful ways. A complex expert system may be combined with elaborate documentation. A hyperdocument which gives guidance on a methodology, for example, may vary its advice by displaying different segments of the methodology for different circumstances.

TYPES OF HYPERDOCUMENT SYSTEMS

There are six generic ways in which hyperdocument systems could be used.

1. **Macro literary systems.** It has long since been proposed that computer networks should support scientific and literary papers with interdocument links so that all publishing, references, collaboration, and criticism takes place within the network. Elab-

orate schemes have been proposed to support the reviewing and criticism of papers. Such hypertext networks would be very valuable for researchers.

It is, however, difficult to establish schemes which require large numbers of organizations to collaborate. Most of today's hyperdocuments are those which can be built by one organization or one individual.

2. **Collections of documents.** Some organizations publish collections of documents in electronic form, with common indexing. These include articles from the trade press, reviews, and technical literature. It is useful to employ hyperlinks to cross-reference such collections and link them to glossaries or tutorials. The hyperdocument system can help the user browse through large bodies of information and can aid him in finding what is useful to him. Where one organization writes multiple documents, much time can be saved by employing hyperlinks to a common set of building blocks which include diagrams, a glossary, a set of tutorials on basic concepts, tables, components descriptions, an acronym list, and references.

3. **Problem exploration tools.** Computer tools exist which help an author organize material by building links among many disconnected ideas and generally structuring the ideas. Such tools may be part of a hyperdocument authoring system or may be an independent "idea processor."

4. **Interrelated sets of information.** Some bodies of information consist of many diverse items which become much more useful when they are associated. In police work, for example, a computer holds detailed descriptions of crimes, criminals, and suspects. It is helpful to link these to help detectives associate crimes or incidents which may relate to the same person or organization. A computer may help identify a common modus operandi.

The author maintains a model of future technology in which the evolution of one technology effects many other technologies, machines, applications, and businesses. The model requires a complex set of hyperlinks to explore the possible implication of technology evolution.

5. **Large and complex documents.** Most organizations use large and complex documents, including procedure manuals, regulations, methodologies, manuals for maintaining complex equipment, documentation for software, and so on. Many of these bulky collections of paper have been converted to electronic form. CD-ROM technology is particularly useful for this. Most large documents are far more usable when built in hyperdocument form so that the user can navigate through them at high speed, electronically opening and closing sections of the document and following links designed to help solve his problems. The challenge is to design the document to take maximum advantage of computerized techniques.

6. **Intelligent documents.** There are many valuable uses of products which combine the ideas of hypermedia and artificial intelligence. Artificial intelligence is concerned with the representation and processing of knowledge. A major type of application of artificial intelligence is the building of expert systems. Expertise is often conveyed in documents; so there is a natural fit between the technology of expert systems and the technology of hyperdocuments.

Hyperdocuments which encapsulate expertise may be used to aid in the maintenance and repair of complex machines or software, diagnosis of complex problems, choice of software or other products, system configuration, computer-based self-education, customization of methodologies, and so on.

There are other types of systems which should combine hyperdocument technology with other forms of computing. These are discussed in Chapter 3.

PARTICULARLY VALUE APPLICATIONS

A great diversity of applications are discussed in hypertext literature. Some of these are appealing but too difficult to implement as yet—for example, networks for criticism of academic literature. Some are entertaining but of little commercial value. Figure 2.9 lists types of applications that are particularly valuable with today's technology.

To make the types of hyperdocuments in Fig. 2.9 as useful as possible, they need to be designed with a skilled understanding of how to use this powerful new medium effectively. That is the subject of the following chapters.

LARGE DOCUMENTS

Product description manuals
  Bulky manuals for complex products ought to be on media such as CD-ROMs in hyperdocument form, designed to make information easy and fast to find and easy to use. Such documentation can be made much easier to update, and generally much more useful, than bulky paper manuals.

Methodologies
  Complex methodologies are used in many professions, not least in the information systems profession. Paper representations of complex methodologies are bulky, inflexible, difficult to update, and not easy to use. Methodologies should be represented in electronic form with options which are selectable depending on the circumstances and the tools used. Well-designed hyperdocuments greatly enhance the value and usability of complex methodologies.

Procedures and guidelines
  Most professions have procedures and guidelines so complex that many professionals do not know the details they need to. Such procedures and guidelines should be in hyperdocument form where the hyperdocument is designed to aid the professional, leading him to the information he needs at a particular time. Well-designed hyperdocuments can greatly lessen the dangers of malpractice.

Regulations and legal literature
  Government regulations and legal literature are often so bulky and complex that civil servants and lawyers take much time searching for information they need. Often they are unaware of items that are important to them. Such regulations and literature should be in intelligent hyperdocuments formatted to give the maximum help to the user.

Figure 2.9 Particularly valuable hyperdocument applications.

(Continued)

INTELLIGENT DOCUMENTS

How-to-use manuals
Intelligent documentation should be designed to translate user concerns into appropriate actions, showing users how to use products for particular purposes and how to solve problems.

Context-sensitive HELP
The manuals for all software ought to be in hyperdocument form. Pressing the HELP key (normally Function Key 1) should link to that part of the hyperdocument which is immediately useful. The hyperdocument may be user-sensitive so that it adapts its guidance to the skill and knowledge of the user.

Computer-based training
Intelligent hyperdocuments are valuable for computer-based training in which the computer is programmed to steadily build up the student's knowledge, testing him where appropriate. The computer retains a record of what the student has learnt and adapts its behavior accordingly.

Self-education services
Intelligent professionals, who already have much knowledge of a subject but who need to enhance their knowledge, often find computer-based training and linear video tapes slow and boring. Instead they need hyperdocuments through which they can navigate at high speed to the segments that interest them.

Expert systems for selection
It is often necessary to make choices among many alternatives, for example, selecting software, selecting options, building blocks, components, investments, techniques, sales arguments, etc. Sometimes systems have to be configured with complex constraints. Hyperdocument systems can be built containing the choice with arguments and links to the details necessary to examine the choice.

Diagnosis and repair hyperdocuments
As illustrated in Figures 2.3 to 2.6, a hyperdocument can be specifically designed to guide its user in the diagnosis of problems and the taking of appropriate corrective action. Expert diagnosis skills can be built into the document.

COLLECTIONS OF DOCUMENTS

Information services
Many industry services exist in which a large amount of detailed information is kept. This information should be on CD-ROMs with periodic updates (replacement disks). Hyperdocument format should be used to make the information as useful as possible and to enable the user to find the information he needs as quickly as possible. The hyperdocuments should be designed to help address the users' issues and help solve their problems.

Industry technical literature
An industry usually has large numbers of products which professionals need to learn about, compare, and contrast. The products have many concepts in common with one another. Literature for professional guidance should be in hyperdocument form, with links to many common modules of information, and intelligent guidance for the user.

Figure 2.9 (Continued)

Trade press CD-ROMs
   CD-ROMs are sold, with period updates, containing vast numbers of
   articles from the trade press. Hyperdocument software can be used
   to automatically link key words in this mass of text to a glossary
   or tutorial explanations of the words.

Library services
   A library has a large number of books, papers, and documents. Some of
   these, or their abstracts, may be on CD-ROM. References to
   documents exist both in catalogs and in other documents. These
   references may be followed with hyperlinks. The catalog and
   mechanisms for intelligent searching should be in hyperdocument
   form even when the documents are still on paper.

INTERRELATED SETS OF INFORMATION

Complex models
   The author's original reason for needing hyperdocuments was to
   represent a complex model of future technology with large numbers
   of cross-links between one type of technology and another. The
   complexity of the interactions is such that the information could
   not be followed or maintained without hyperdocuments. Other complex
   information with many lateral links is greatly enhanced by building
   it in hyperdocument form.

Police files
   The police have a large amount of information about a large number
   of crimes, criminals, and suspects. Many hyperlinks can be threaded
   through this information to help detectives search for potential
   criminals with a modus operandi or other clues that may help to
   solve a crime.

Figure 2.9 (Continued)

3 HYPERDOCUMENTS COMBINED WITH OTHER COMPUTING FACILITIES

There are many potentially valuable applications in which hyperdocuments are combined with other computing facilities. Examples of such combinations are

- Database applications linked to hyperdocuments
- General computing capabilities linked to hyperdocuments
- Software with hyperdocument HELP facilities
- Hyperdocuments with built-in expert systems

Figure 3.1 lists examples in each category. The combination of hypermedia with other forms of computing is likely to become of great value for many professionals.

DATABASES LINKED TO HYPERMEDIA
Many database systems use conventional database management software and are regularly updated; it would be valuable to connect these databases to hyperdocuments describing the items in the database. In some cases, these databases may be distributed on CD-ROMs.

Use of this in the financial arena, for example, would give investment planners the capability to search for investments which meet certain financial criteria and hyperlink those to corporate reports, analysts' reports, and the recommendations of major investment houses.

Since part of such information changes rapidly and part of it is fairly static, it would make sense to link a time-sharing service to a CD-ROM database.

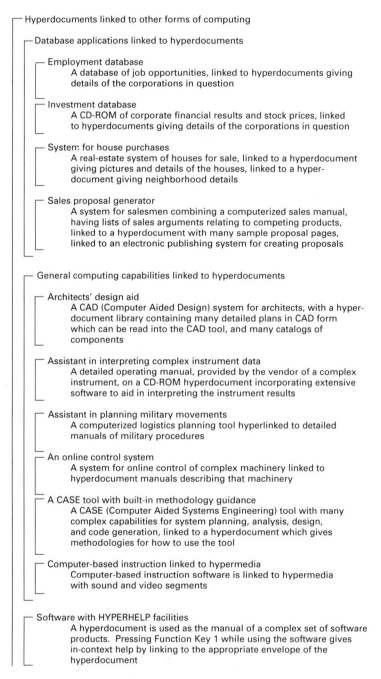

Hyperdocuments linked to other forms of computing

Database applications linked to hyperdocuments

Employment database
A database of job opportunities, linked to hyperdocuments giving details of the corporations in question

Investment database
A CD-ROM of corporate financial results and stock prices, linked to hyperdocuments giving details of the corporations in question

System for house purchases
A real-estate system of houses for sale, linked to a hyperdocument giving pictures and details of the houses, linked to a hyperdocument giving neighborhood details

Sales proposal generator
A system for salesmen combining a computerized sales manual, having lists of sales arguments relating to competing products, linked to a hyperdocument with many sample proposal pages, linked to an electronic publishing system for creating proposals

General computing capabilities linked to hyperdocuments

Architects' design aid
A CAD (Computer Aided Design) system for architects, with a hyperdocument library containing many detailed plans in CAD form which can be read into the CAD tool, and many catalogs of components

Assistant in interpreting complex instrument data
A detailed operating manual, provided by the vendor of a complex instrument, on a CD-ROM hyperdocument incorporating extensive software to aid in interpreting the instrument results

Assistant in planning military movements
A computerized logistics planning tool hyperlinked to detailed manuals of military procedures

An online control system
A system for online control of complex machinery linked to hyperdocument manuals describing that machinery

A CASE tool with built-in methodology guidance
A CASE (Computer Aided Systems Engineering) tool with many complex capabilities for system planning, analysis, design, and code generation, linked to a hyperdocument which gives methodologies for how to use the tool

Computer-based instruction linked to hypermedia
Computer-based instruction software is linked to hypermedia with sound and video segments

Software with HYPERHELP facilities
A hyperdocument is used as the manual of a complex set of software products. Pressing Function Key 1 while using the software gives in-context help by linking to the appropriate envelope of the hyperdocument

Figure 3.1 Examples of hyperdocument technology combined with other forms of computing.

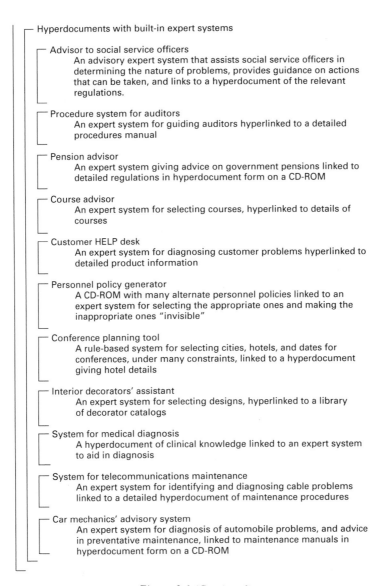

Hyperdocuments with built-in expert systems

Advisor to social service officers
An advisory expert system that assists social service officers in determining the nature of problems, provides guidance on actions that can be taken, and links to a hyperdocument of the relevant regulations.

Procedure system for auditors
An expert system for guiding auditors hyperlinked to a detailed procedures manual

Pension advisor
An expert system giving advice on government pensions linked to detailed regulations in hyperdocument form on a CD-ROM

Course advisor
An expert system for selecting courses, hyperlinked to details of courses

Customer HELP desk
An expert system for diagnosing customer problems hyperlinked to detailed product information

Personnel policy generator
A CD-ROM with many alternate personnel policies linked to an expert system for selecting the appropriate ones and making the inappropriate ones "invisible"

Conference planning tool
A rule-based system for selecting cities, hotels, and dates for conferences, under many constraints, linked to a hyperdocument giving hotel details

Interior decorators' assistant
An expert system for selecting designs, hyperlinked to a library of decorator catalogs

System for medical diagnosis
A hyperdocument of clinical knowledge linked to an expert system to aid in diagnosis

System for telecommunications maintenance
An expert system for identifying and diagnosing cable problems linked to a detailed hyperdocument of maintenance procedures

Car mechanics' advisory system
An expert system for diagnosis of automobile problems, and advice in preventative maintenance, linked to maintenance manuals in hyperdocument form on a CD-ROM

Figure 3.1 (Continued)

COMPUTING CAPABILITIES LINKED TO HYPERDOCUMENTS

Hyperdocument/computing facility linkages will be effective for many applications:

- Tools for design, planning, analysis, spreadsheet manipulation, and so on may be linked with hyperdocuments.

- Computer-based training software may incorporate hypermedia with sound and video segments. Computer-based training may be linked to a hyperdocument library giving information about products.

- Hyperdocuments describing complex methodologies may be connected to the software tools used to implement what the methodologies describe.

- Software for complex instruments, machinery, or process control may be linked with an electronic manual which describes how to use such facilities.

- Software for logistics planning and the management of complex operation should be connected to hyperdocuments which describe those operations.

HYPER-HELP

It is desirable for software vendors to deliver the documentation for their software in electronic form. This is less expensive than paper documentation.

It should also enable the user of the software to display at any instant the documentation which might solve his problems or enable him to learn more about using the software. To achieve this, the software manual should be in hyperdocument form, and the HELP key (on most machines, Function Key 1) should cause the appropriate part of it to be displayed.

The term *in-context help* is employed to mean that a software user receives help about the activity he is currently trying to perform. To achieve this, a link should be made to the hyperdocument envelope relating to that activity.

KNOWLEDGE AND KNOWLEDGE BASES

Much knowledge used in the running of enterprises resides in the heads of employees and is not formally recorded. Mechanics know how to diagnose subtle problems, auditors know where to look for evidence of fraud, shop-floor expediters know how to work around breakdowns and meet their production schedules. In IBM's microelectronics factories, the proportion of faulty chips produced sometimes drifts upward. Certain experts who have spent years in the factory know how to improve the yield. The process by which they do this has been referred to in IBM as "alchemy," but it works. IBM built an expert system to capture this subtle expertise, and that system now saves IBM more than $30 million per year in one plant alone [1].

An important and valuable use of computers is the recording of knowledge so that, instead being tacitly or verbally transmitted, it is transmitted via electronic interfaces. This enables such knowledge to be recorded, cloned, steadily added to until it becomes an impressive body of knowledge which can be stored on disks or transmitted over distances and put to use to help solve problems.

The discipline of artificial intelligence is concerned with encoding knowledge and storing it in knowledge bases. Knowledge bases associate data with rules in such a way that a computer can use the rules to draw inferences. Expert systems are an encapsulation of knowledge. Their user interacts with them so that the knowledge is used in rule-based processing to come to conclusions such as how to repair a machine, what software to select or what a production schedule should be.

NONPROCESSABLE KNOWLEDGE

Because knowledge bases and knowledge processing are at the heart of most work on artificial intelligence, there is a tendency to equate the concept of "knowledge" with rule-based processing and formal methods of encoding knowledge. It is important to understand that this is a limited form of "knowledge."

Most human knowledge would be very difficult to encapsulate with rules and today's knowledge-base structures. A rule-based system applies to a narrow, well-bounded domain of knowledge with precise objects and actions. If an expert system ventures the tiniest step beyond its domain, it plunges into an abyss of nonsense. Although rule-based systems give us a new type of power in processing knowledge, most human knowledge will continue to be stored in the form of text and diagrams which humans can use but machines cannot.

Textbooks and hyperdocuments derive their expressive power from their ability to refer to a vast diversity of conceptual frameworks and to use metaphors, similes, analogies, diagrams, images, and rhetorical devices which a computer cannot process. Computers today cannot exhibit the common sense and world knowledge that we use all the time in literature.

Human knowledge can be stored in computer systems in two separate ways:

- Formal knowledge encoding, rule-based processing, and algorithms
- Hypertext and hypermedia

Both ways of storing knowledge are very useful. Computerized knowledge can be put to work by vast numbers of people, and knowledge stored in computers tends to grow as different people add to it.

HYPERDOCUMENTS WITH BUILT-IN EXPERT SYSTEMS

There are many problems that need both the formality of rule-based processing and the informality of hyperdocuments. We need software which combines these capabilities.

The Ford Motor Company, for example, is concerned with improving its service-bay diagnostics. To do so, it is working with an artificial intelligence firm to build an expert system for diagnosing problems. This system can reason about faults and symptoms and suggest diagnostic tests. At the same time, Ford is building a hyperdocument system to store and link a large quantity of text and graphics from its service manuals. When the expert system suggests repair procedures, the mechanics will call up relevant text and graphics from the enormous online hyperdocument store.

As in many other such situations, the Ford mechanics are highly trained, but the knowledge needed for maintenance is vast and is changing rapidly. The system aids them both substantially with its rule-based diagnosis and its ability to call up the requisite text and diagrams.

There are innumerable potential applications of hyperdocuments with expert systems built into them, combining different ways of computerizing human knowledge. The bottom (fourth) part of Fig. 3.1 lists types of hyperdocuments with built-in expert systems.

As society's machines and organizations become ever more complex, it will be increasingly important to provide carefully selected information to people working at every level. Humans will need to be able to interact with expert systems and be able to access and interpret information in accordance with their circumstances and skills.

PART II HOW TO ORGANIZE HYPERDOCUMENTS

4 CLARITY IN HYPERDOCUMENT STRUCTURES

INTRODUCTION This and the following chapters describe how to create hyperdocuments that are as clear and valuable to the user as possible. As in other fields the computer can cause chaos unless careful analysis is done of how to put its power to good use. Amateurish hyperdocuments are a disaster.

As we create guidelines to describe what techniques work best for creating hyperdocuments, we discover that much of the advice would also be valuable to the writer of paper reports or textbooks. Hypermedia demand clear thinking and good structures. The same clear thinking would improve paper-based authoring. I have culled illustrations from some of the many textbooks I have written and have concluded that if they were rewritten with hypermedia discipline, they would be better textbooks.

THE NEED FOR CLARITY The author of a hyperdocument builds modules of text and connects them together. He may build tables and pictures and connect them to the text. He devises menus and pointers so that the reader can navigate around the document.

The single most important aspect of creating a hyperdocument is that it must be designed with a clear structure. It is only too easy to create a spaghettilike mess in which, although the author likes it, the reader will become rapidly lost. In practice, even hyperdocuments as short as one book chapter are confusing when created haphazardly. It is a common experience for a person who has used a hyperdocument multiple times to be surprised by the discovery of some valuable item which eluded him previously. He wonders what other pearls of wisdom are hidden in the maze.

CLEARLY VISIBLE STRUCTURE   In a hypertext system, it is possible to have links between any piece of information and any other piece. This allows ideas to be associated in valuable ways. However, it tempts an unskilled author to create a mess of links in which the reader quickly becomes lost. He often does not find all of the items that could be of value to him and may have difficulty revisiting items that he wants to see again. Unlike in a book, nothing is visible until the reader navigates to it, and navigation must be done via the small screen of the computer.

To create good-quality hypertext, it is necessary to impose a clear structure on information and make the structure visible to the user. The most commonly used form of structure is a hierarchy.

ENVELOPES   A hyperdocument is divided into chunks of information. These chunks of information are organized into structures. Each chunk of information can be thought of as being in a container. We shall refer to this container as an *envelope*.

Each envelope should have a title. When the envelope is closed, the viewer can read its title. In most cases, when the envelope is opened, the viewer can see its contents.

One envelope may have other envelopes inside it. These envelopes may, themselves, have other envelopes inside them. There is thus a hierarchy of envelopes. A hyperdocument version of this book would have an envelope for each figure and for each chunk of text which has a margin heading. The text you are reading would be in an envelope entitled "ENVELOPES," for example. That would reside, with other envelopes, in a larger envelope entitled "CHAPTER 4: CLARITY IN HYPERDOCUMENT STRUCTURES." That would reside in a still larger envelope entitled "PART II: HOW TO ORGANIZE HYPERDOCUMENTS." That resides in the outermost envelope, which corresponds to the book as a whole.

HIERARCHIES   Envelopes are organized into structures. The most common form of structure is a hierarchy (envelopes within envelopes within envelopes).

Figure 4.1 shows a hierarchy, which might be the structure of a paper document. The segments of a document are numbered. Software can number them automatically and renumber them when the author makes a change.

A book or a technical report has a single hierarchy, which is summarized in its table of contents. A hyperdocument may have multiple hierarchies which are interlinked. For example, a document about the future of computing may have one hierarchy relating to technology, one to applications, and one to social

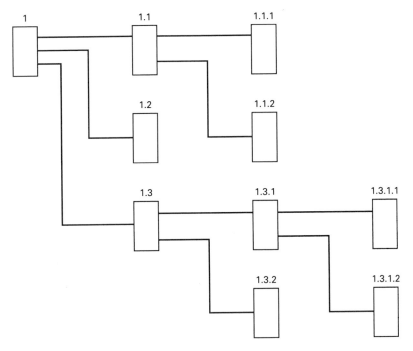

Figure 4.1   Hierarchical structure with segments (automatically) numbered.

impact. There may be multiple cross-links connecting these hierarchies. There may be one set of such hierarchies for 5 years in the future, one for 10 years, and one for 20 years. The viewer may start by looking at a diagram which makes this structure clear.

OVERLAP AMONG HIERARCHIES   In a book, each chapter or piece of information appears in the table of contents only once. In a hyperdocument, an item may be referred to by multiple hierarchies or in different places in the same hierarchy. Many different pages may have buttons linking to the same item.

Figure 4.2 shows two such hierarchies. There are, however, two links connecting the hierarchies. Segment 1.3.1.2 is a subsegment of segment 2.2.1. Segment 1.2 has a subordinate structure consisting of segments 2.1.1, 2.1.1.1 and 2.1.1.2. A segment which gives an explanation of an idea might be linked to many other segments. It is a target of buttons in different places. An entire hierarchy might be used to explain an idea and, so, be the target of buttons in many other hierarchies.

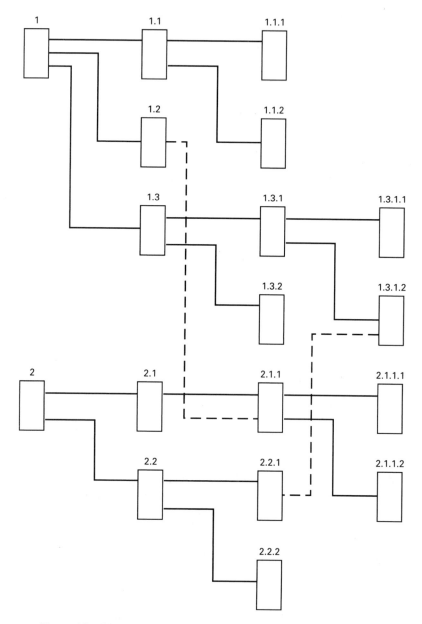

Figure 4.2 Two hierarchical structures with cross-links between them.

NETWORK STRUCTURE

A hierarchy with no cross-links, as in Fig. 4.1, is sometimes called a tree structure. Multiple hierarchies with cross-links among them constitute a network structure, as in Fig. 4.2.

A network structure built in an unruly fashion is like spaghetti. It becomes difficult to grow and maintain. Worse, it is difficult for the reader who views it via a computer screen to visualize the structure, know where he is, and navigate around the structure. A hypertext viewer in a spaghettilike structure is like a rat in a maze.

Hypertext should be built with clearly visible hierarchies and well-organized links. The links sometimes make connections within one hierarchy and sometimes span separate hierarchies. The links sometimes connect separate documents.

The reader must be able to see the hierarchies showing titles, like a table of contents.

OTHER ORGANIZING PARADIGMS

In other cases an overview structure may be different from a hierarchy. It could be a matrix or a three-sided pyramid with pointers to text. The text pointed to may, itself, be organized into hierarchies.

If the structure around which the document is organized is different from the tree structure, there should be a clear diagram of the structure. The reader should see that diagram first. The diagram is the highest node in a hierarchy like block 1 in Fig. 4.1.

If a matrix, a pyramid, or other chart is used to structure the document, we say that the chart is an organizing "paradigm." The word "paradigm" means a pattern or structure.

VISUAL REPRESENTATION OF ENVELOPES

The hyperdocument reader needs to see a drawing of the envelopes and have the capability to open and close envelopes by interacting with their screen representation. The software should provide user-friendly techniques for building, manipulating, and navigating through envelope structures.

An appealing way to draw and interact with envelopes is that used in the Macintosh Hypercard. Here, an envelope is referred to as a "card." The card looks like cards in a rotary card file, and each card is represented by an icon (a drawing about half an inch wide), which has a title written by it. Figure 4.3 shows Hypercard icons. When the Macintosh user clicks the mouse on an icon, it "opens" to fill most of the screen, displaying its contents. Its contents include icons representing other cards. These act as hyperdocument *buttons*. There can

Home Card

Figure 4.3   Hypercard icons.

be cards within cards and links between separate cards. The user can navigate among cards by clicking the mouse on icons.

The Hypercard user can have "stacks" of such cards, which can contain text, images, sound, and programs. He can navigate sequentially through the stack or hyperlink at any stage to a different card. There can be cards within cards within cards—representing a hierarchy—and there can be any-to-any links among cards. The user can insert new cards into the stack at any place as he could with a rotary card file.

Most cards have the following icons:

⟵   :   Go back to the previous card.

⟶   :   Go to the next card.

🏠   :   Home card.

Clicking on the home card takes you to the opening card—from which you can link to any stack. This is the jumping-off point for all navigation through the stacks.

BRACKET DIAGRAMS

Icons like those on Hypercards seem ideal for manipulating and organizing collections of notes and cards. For navigating through large documents, a bracket diagram is more useful.

ENVELOPE DIAGRAMS

Good hypertext software provides user-friendly techniques for building, manipulating and navigating through hierarchies and their cross-links. Figure 4.4 shows an envelope diagram that corresponds to Fig. 4.1. This is a useful way of representing a hierarchy. The outermost envelope contains other envelopes; these, in turn, contain envelopes and so on until the lowest-level envelope. The lowest-level envelopes contain text, diagrams, images, or, possibly, animated diagrams, speech, or television. A hierarchy (or tree structure) thus consists of envelopes within envelopes within envelopes, ...

It is convenient to draw an envelope diagram on a computer screen by showing only the left-hand sides of the envelopes. Figure 4.5 is an abbreviated form of Fig. 4.4. The reader can scroll up and down an envelope diagram,

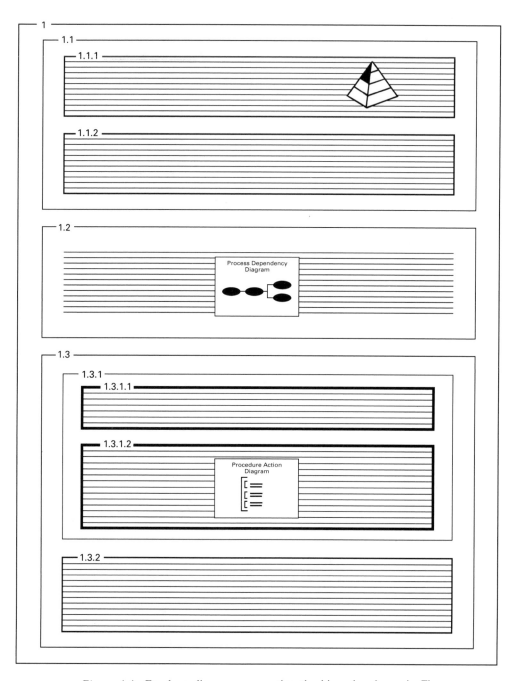

Figure 4.4 Envelope diagram representing the hierarchy shown in Figure 4.1.

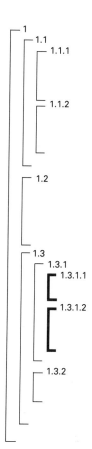

Figure 4.5 The top of each envelope on an envelope diagram indicates the contents of the envelope. It is convenient to draw an envelope diagram showing only the left sides of the envelopes, which are called *brackets*. This diagram is the left side of Figure 4.4. This type of diagram is called a *bracket diagram*.

quickly opening and closing envelopes. The line at the top of each envelope is a title of a segment of information, as shown in Fig. 4.6. It indicates the contents of the envelope.

The lowest-level envelopes (the rightmost envelopes) are called basic envelopes because they are not further subdivided. They are the leaf nodes of the tree structure. These basic envelopes contain the substance of the hyperdocument, in the form of text, diagrams, or other information.

THE CREATION OF LINKS

A hyperdocument may have multiple envelope diagrams which are interlinked. As discussed earlier, the connections which enable the reader to traverse hyperdocuments consist of a button, a link, and a target. When an author builds a

Figure 4.6 The top of each bracket on a bracket diagram indicates the contents of the envelope.

hypertext link, it is useful if he can see both the button and the target on the screen. The hypertext authoring system should display two scrollable windows for this purpose, one showing the button and one showing the target. The author can then be sure that he is building the desired link.

OPENING AND CLOSING ENVELOPES   To make a hierarchy visible on the screen, items on it may be opened or closed as the viewer requires. The viewer may press the OPEN key continuously and open all the envelopes within a selected envelope. Conversely, the viewer may press the CLOSE key continuously, closing the whole hierarchy of envelopes. This ability to open and close envelopes at the touch of a key is a particularly valuable way to manipulate hyperdocuments.

The user may move the cursor to any envelope on the screen and issue a CLOSE command. The envelope then shrinks to one line. To show that the line is a contracted envelope, the line is preceded by two or three dots. Two dots indicate that an envelope with no inner envelopes has been contracted. Three dots indicate the contraction of an envelope which itself contains envelopes.

Thus, in the following diagram,

```
┌─ NOEL COWARD
│
│   . . INTRODUCTION
│
│   . . . SHORT STORIES
│
│   . . . NOVELS
│
│   . . . SONGS
│
└─  . . . PLAYS
```

the dots indicate that INTRODUCTION is an envelope with no inner envelopes; SHORT STORIES, NOVELS, SONGS, and PLAYS are each envelopes which themselves contain other envelopes.

The reader might move the cursor to SONGS and give the OPEN command. The result is as follows:

```
┌─ NOEL COWARD
│  . . INTRODUCTION
│  . . . SHORT STORIES
│  . . . NOVELS
│  ┌─ SONGS
│  │   . . . SOME DAY I'LL FIND YOU
│  │   . . . MRS. WORTHINGTON
│  │   . . . A ROOM WITH A VIEW
│  │   . . . THE STATELY HOMES OF ENGLAND
│  │   . . . DON'T LET'S BE BEASTLY TO THE GERMANS
│  │   . . . MAD DOGS AND ENGLISHMEN
│  └─  . . . THE PARTY'S OVER NOW
│
│   . . .PLAYS
└─
```

Moving the cursor to MAD DOGS AND ENGLISHMEN and again saying OPEN opens that envelope, as follows:

Pointing to COMMENTARY BY NOEL COWARD and OPENing the envelope gives the following result [1]:

```
. . . DON'T LET'S BE BEASTLY TO THE GERMANS

  MAD DOGS AND ENGLISHMEN

  . . HISTORICAL NOTE

    COMMENTARY BY NOEL COWARD

         Oddly enough, one of the few songs I ever wrote that
         came to me in a setting appropriate to its content was
         "Mad Dogs and Englishmen."  This was conceived and
         executed during a two-thousand-mile car drive from
         Hanoi in Tonkin to the Siamese border.  True, the only
         white people to be seen were French, but one can't have
         everything.

         "Mad Dogs and Englishmen" was originally sung in
         America by Beatrice Lilly in "The Little Show."  In
         "Words and Music," Romney Brent sang it as a missionary
         in one of Britain's tropical colonies.  Since then, I have
         sung it myself ad nauseam.  On one occasion it achieved
         international significance.  This was a dinner party given
         by Mr. Winston Churchill on board H.M.S. Prince of Wales
         in honor of President Roosevelt on the evening following
         the signing of the Atlantic Charter.  From an eye-witness
         description of the scene, it appears that the two world leaders
         became involved in a heated argument as to whether "In
         Bangkok at twelve o'clock they foam at the mouth and run"
         came at the end of the first refrain or at the end of the second.
         President Roosevelt held firmly to the latter view and refused
         to budge even under the impact of Churchillian rhetoric.  In
         this he was right and when, a little while later, I asked Mr.
         Churchill about the incident, he admitted defeat like a man.

  . . . MUSIC

  . . . WORDS

  . . AUDIO

. . . THE PARTY'S OVER NOW

. . . PLAYS
```

Large hierarchies may be shrunk to one line by pressing CLOSE repeatedly. A book structure may be shrunk to one line showing the book title and then OPENed once to show the chapter titles. OPENing again for the book as a whole reveals the subheadings within every chapter. Alternatively, the cursor may be moved and one chapter OPENed.

**THE SAME
ENVELOPE IN
MULTIPLE PLACES**

A network structure such as that in Fig. 4.2 can be represented by envelope diagrams—envelopes within envelopes within envelopes—but some of the envelopes must be in more than one place. Envelope 1.3.1.2 in Fig. 4.2, for example, is inside envelopes 1.3.1 and also 2.2.1. Envelope 2.1.1 (which contains envelopes 2.1.1.1 and 2.1.1.2) is inside both envelopes 2.1 and 1.2.

When an envelope is in multiple places, like this, its contents are not duplicated. Instead, there are software links to one set of contents (as in Fig. 4.2). If the contents of envelope 2.1.1 are modified, this in effect changes the contents of 2.1 and 1.2. This permits one piece of text or one set of ideas to be used in multiple places.

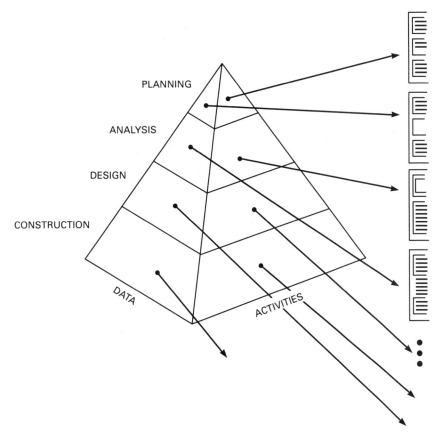

Figure 4.7 The document may be organized around a structure which is diagrammed (in this case, a pyramid). The reader should see this diagram first. The diagram should have explanatory labels and a caption. Buttons on the diagram should point to the hypertext hierarchies.

MIXING HIERARCHICAL AND NONHIERARCHICAL ORGANIZATION

We have indicated that the organization of a hyperdocument may be based on a diagram other than a hierarchy. It is often very useful to have a picture which helps the reader visualize something and then relate parts of the picture to sections of the document. The parts of the picture may be linked to envelope diagrams as shown in Fig. 4.7.

An envelope may contain a picture. That picture may have displayable buttons which link to other envelopes. Text in an envelope may point to a picture; a picture may have buttons which point to other envelopes. Envelope diagrams and other pictures are thus intermixed. Hierarchies and other paradigms are used together.

NUMBERING THE SECTIONS OF THE DOCUMENT

An envelope diagram could represent a simple structure such as a list, a multilevel hierarchy, or many multilevel hierarchies.

Hyperdocuments often consist of many multilevel hierarchies. The author of the document arranges the hierarchies into a sequence even though they may not be read sequentially. The envelopes in the document can be numbered automatically by the software. First, a sequence number is placed on each top-level envelope:

Then the envelopes in each hierarchy are numbered, numbering the leftmost envelopes first and processing downward, then the next-to-leftmost and so on, like this:

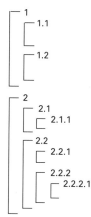

NUMBERING THE DIAGRAMS

In an envelope structure, diagrams are inside the envelopes. It is recommended that no envelope should have more than one diagram. Each diagram has its own envelope. Two diagrams represent two sets of thoughts, and these should be in two envelopes.

Diagram numbers can be the numbers of their envelopes; hence, they can be assigned automatically.

LEAVING NOTES

It is valuable to have a mechanism for leaving notes in a hyperdocument. These notes may not remain in the final version. The author should be able to leave notes for himself. Two or more cooperating authors should be able to leave notes for one another. Reviewers or friends should be able to leave notes for the author. Copy editors should be able to leave notes and make recommended text modifications adjacent to the original text. There should be a means of knowing such notes exist and finding them.

The reader may also leave notes and bookmarks or may color the text, just as he does with a book. The same mechanisms can be used for authors' notes and readers' notes.

TYPES OF ENVELOPES

A hyperdocument can have multiple types of envelopes. The following are possible types:

- **Text.** The envelope contains anything created with the text character set. It is normally scrollable vertically.
- **Diagrams.** The envelope contains color diagrams created with a "paint" or "draw" program or with software which creates charts from numbers.

- **Images.** The envelope contains bit-mapped images read in from a scanner. There may be no distinction between an envelope containing a *diagram* and one containing an *image*. On the other hand, there may be a special envelope with automatic links to particular paint or draw software.

- **Animation.** An envelope executes software which creates the appearance of a moving image. Animation packages which do this are available.

- **Sound.** The envelope plays digitized sound—speech or music. This can be combined with an image on the screen.

- **Video.** The envelope displays a televisionlike image on the screen of the computer. It may occupy the whole screen or a small window. It may be generated from the computer disk or from an external laser disk.

- **External television.** Opening the envelope results in a sequence being played on a television set which is separate from the computer. It may initiate the display of a television sequence from a laser disk.

- **Program.** Opening the envelope initiates the execution of a program. The program may carry out a dialogue with the viewer. It may display the results of calculations. It may be an expert system.

Because there are many possible types of software, there may be multiple types of software envelope. The viewer may think that the envelope "contains" a program. In fact, the envelope is merely a gateway to other software. It is desirable that hyperdocuments software provide an OPEN interface to other software.

Hyperdocument software must know what is in an envelope so that it can take the requisite action when the envelope is opened. It must recognize multiple types of envelope. An envelope is, thus, an *object* of a specified type and has certain properties.

VISUAL APPEARANCE OF ENVELOPES

It is desirable that the user have an indication of what is in an envelope before he opens it. A diagram should be used on which the reader sees the title of the envelope before opening it. It is usually desirable to also indicate the type of envelope—whether it contains a diagram or video, for example. This could be done by the author who includes that information with the title. It may be done automatically by the software. Different icons or colors may indicate different types of envelopes.

The author may be able to indicate that certain envelopes are particularly important. The reader, also, may be able to mark the envelope to indicate that it is special to him. This facility can be useful to the reader of large or complex hyperdocuments.

5 CLARITY IN HYPERDOCUMENT IDEAS

SEQUENCE The author of a book or television program usually expects the audience to progress through the material sequentially with only minor lapses or digressions. Because the author is in control of sequence, he can build up his audience's knowledge a step at a time. The author of a hyperdocument has no such luxury. The reader or viewer will skip, follow links, and open and close envelopes as his fancy takes him.

The reader of a good hyperdocument finds it useful to be able to follow links directly to subjects that interest him. If he is reading something which contains an unfamiliar concept, it is useful to be able to flash across a hyperlink to material which explains that concept and then come back. This process only works well when the targets of such hyperlinks are self-contained so that different readers at different places in the document can use them.

NUGGETS Success in authoring hyperdocuments, then, depends on dividing the subject matter into self-contained fragments. We will refer to a self-contained fragment of information as a *nugget*. If removed from its document, a nugget can usually be understood in its own right.

It is useful to distinguish three main types of nuggets:

- **Basic building blocks.** These are lowest-level envelopes containing one idea. They are not necessarily relevant when out of context; therefore, they may not by themselves be targets of hyperlinks.
- **Diagram units.** These are lowest-level envelopes which contain a diagram and, possibly, some associated text. The diagram should have a self-explanatory caption so that it is meaningful out of context.

- **Concept units.** These are explanations of basic concepts which are valid regardless of context. They may be hyperlinked to/from any document.

A basic building block may or may not, by itself, be the target of hyperlinks. Concept units and diagram units are intended to be targets of hyperlinks. A concept unit may be hyperlinked to/from multiple documents.

The understanding of what is and what is not a target is important for the maintenance of hyperdocuments (as discussed in Chapter 15, "Maintenance").

BASIC BUILDING BLOCKS

The lowest-level (innermost) building unit should contain a single idea. It is the *basic building block*. In this book, the units of text with a margin heading (like this one entitled "Basic Building Blocks") are the basic blocks.

In general, it is recommended that the innermost envelope should extend over not more than three computer screens. It often extends for only a few lines on the screen. The authoring software might caution the author when he creates a bottom-level envelope, the contents of which are too large. Sometimes the bottom-level envelope has to be large—for example, when it contains a previously existing document which cannot be changed or subdivided.

CONCEPT UNIT

The material which explains a basic concept is called a *concept unit*. In the explanation of a concept there might be several important ideas. There should be an *index of concept units*.

A concept unit may consist of one building block or may contain many building blocks. In other words, it may be a bottom-level envelope or may contain other envelopes. The concept unit may, thus, be subdivisible, whereas the building block is not.

A concept unit might include other concept units, as shown in Fig. 5.1. It might contain envelopes which are concept units and envelopes which are not. In this chapter, concept units are drawn with thicker-level envelopes than are other envelopes so that the viewer can clearly identify them.

Index of Concept Units

Because concept units may be targets of hyperlinks from multiple documents, it is useful for authoring software to build and maintain an index of concept units. In many of my textbooks written years ago I placed an index of basic concepts at the front of the book, after the table of contents. This proved to be very helpful. Figure 5.2 shows the entries in the index of basic concepts from the book *Telecommunications and the Computer* [1]. That book is not *about* the items in Fig. 5.2, but these concepts had to be understood to follow the arguments of the

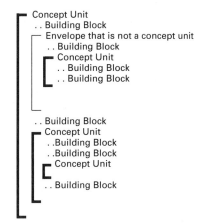

Figure 5.1　A concept unit may contain multiple building blocks. A basic building block is the lowest-level building unit. A concept unit may contain other concept units. Concept units are drawn with thick envelopes in this diagram. A building block may be a diagram or, possibly, an image, animated diagram, speech segment, video segment, or computer program.

book. In a hyperdocument about developments in telecommunications, there should be a concept unit explaining each of the basic concepts in Fig. 5.2.

　　Once an author declares an envelope as a concept unit, an index entry for that concept unit can be added *automatically* to the index of concept units. The concept unit must have a title which is self-explanatory when that unit is removed from its current context.

Example of Concept Unit

One of the entries in the index of basic concepts of *Telecommunications and the Computer* is "packet switching." This is an important concept unit. An explanation of packet switching is quite complex and needs, itself, to contain other concept units. Figure 5.3 shows a structure that is appropriate for the concept unit "packet switching."

　　In Fig. 5.3 the thicker brackets represent concept units. A line which starts with two dots is a heading for one single envelope. Some of the envelopes in the hierarchy of Fig. 5.3 are not themselves concept units and so are not in the index of concept units.

　　Some of the items in Fig. 5.3 that are not marked as concept units are very important, for example, "CCITT Recommendation X.25" and "OSI Model." These are both major subjects but are dealt with elsewhere. The packet switching concept unit contains only a summary of the CCITT Recommendation X.25 and the OSI Model, and both of these summaries have buttons which hyperlink to concept units elsewhere which explain those topics in detail, perhaps giving lengthy documentation from the standards bodies. It will be noted that each thick bracket in Fig. 5.3 has a title which is self-explanatory when removed

Accoustical coupler
Adoptive routing
Amplitude modulation
Analog transmission
ARPANET
ARQ System
Arrival curve
ASCII Code
Asynchronous transmission
AT&T
Attenuation
Attenuation, in radio transmission
Attenuation constant
Attenuation distortion
Availability of lines

Bandwidth
Baseband signaling
Baud
Baudot code
Bell System
Bias distortion
Bipolar signaling
Buffer

Capacitance
Carrier frequency
Carterphone ruling
CCITT
CCITT International Alphabet
Channel capacity
Circuit switching
Coaxial cable
Common carriers (U.S.)
Common carriers, specialized
Common carriers, value added
Common channel signaling
Communication lines
Communications Act of 1934 (U.S.)
Compandor
Comsat
Concentrator
Conditioning, C&D
Conditioning, line
Control characteristics
Control signals

Control signals, data system
Control signals, telephone system
Crosstalk

D.A.A.
Data codes
Data collection system
Datapac service (Canada)
Dataset (modem)
Data transmission
Data transmission systems (categories)
DATRAN
DDS
Decibel
Delay distortion
Delivery time
Demand assignment
Dialing
Dialogue, man-computer
Digital Data Service (U.S.)
Digital transmission
Direct access adaptor
Direct current signaling
Distortion, delay
Distortion, fortuitous
Distortion, harmonic
Distortion, systematic
Distributed intelligence
Double current telegraph signal

Earth return circuit
Earth station
Echo
Echo check
Echo suppressors
EFT (Electronic Fund Transfer)
Electromagnetic spectrum
Electronic switching systems
End-to-end signaling
Entropy
Error correcting codes
Error detecting codes
Error ratios
Error treatment
Escape character
ESS #1

Figure 5.2 Index of Basic Concepts from *Telecommunications and the Computer* [1].

ESS #2

FCC (Federal Communications Commission) (U.S.)

Fortuitous distortion

Fourier analysis

Four-wire circuit

Frequency

Frequency division multiplexing

Frequency modulation

Full duplex

Gaussian noise

Grade of service

GT&E

Guard band

Half-duplex

Hertz

Impulse noise

In-band signaling

Independent telephone companies

Inductance

Information theory

INTELSAT

Interactive system

Interconnect industry

Interconnection

International alphabet #2

International alphabet #5

Intertoll trunk

ITT

ITU

Kelvin's law

Leakage

Leased line

Line conditioning

Loading

Local loops

Loop check

Loops, local

Man-computer dialogue

M.C.I.

Measured use service

Message switching

Message switching systems

MF

Microwave fading

Microwave radio links

Modem

Modem standards (CCITT)

Modulat ion
  amplitude
  data
  frequency
  phase
  voice

Multifrequency signaling (MF)

Multiplexing

Murray code

Network, circuit switched
  message switched
  packet switched
  store and forward

Network control programs

Neutral signaling

Noise

Noninteractive system

Office of Telecommunications Policy (OTP) (U.S.)

Offline system

Online system

Optical fiber cable

OTP (U.S.)

Out-band signaling

PABX

Packet

Packet switched network

Packet switching

PAM

PBX

PCI

PCM

Peak/average transmission ratio

Phantom circuit

Phase distortion

Phase modulation

Point-to-point signaling

Polar signaling

Polynomial code

Private automatic branch exchange

Private branch exchange (*see* PBX)

Figure 5.2   (Continued)

(Continued)

Propagation delay
Propagation delay, for satellite
Propagation time
Pulse amplitude modulation (PAM)
Pulse code modulation (PCM)

RCA
Regenerative repeater
Resource sharing network
Response time
Ringing tone

Satellite channel (unique properties)
Satellites, communication
Satellites, geosynchronous
Shannon
Signaling:
   asynchronous
   baseband
   bipolar
   common channel
   direct current
   duplex
   end-to-end
   half duplex
   in-band
   MF
   neutral
   polar
   out-band
   point-to-point
   simplex
   single current (telegraph)
   start-stop
   supervisory, control
   synchronous
Signal-to-noise ratio
Simplex circuit
Simplex transmission
SPADE
Spectrum diagram
Start-stop transmission
Step-by-step switching
Store-and-forward network
Strowger switch
Superposing
Supervisory signals

Switching facilities (telephone
  company)
Switched line
Switching office hierarchy
Synchronous satellite
Synchronous transmission

T-1 carrier
Tariff
TASI
TCTS (Canada)
Telenet, Inc.
TELESAT (Canada)
Teleprinter
Teletype machine
Telex
Terminal
Terminal, buffered, intelligent
Thermal noise
Tie line, tie trunk
Time division multiplexing
Time division switching
Time sharing system
Time sharing telecommunications
  facilities
Toll connecting trunk
Touchtone dialing
Transmission:
  analog
  digital
  media
  speeds
  systems chart (North America)
Transponder
Trunk circuits
Two-wire circuit
TWX

Unipolar signaling
US ITA

Value added common carriers

Wave guide
WESTAR
Western Electric
Western Union
White noise

Figure 5.2   (Continued)

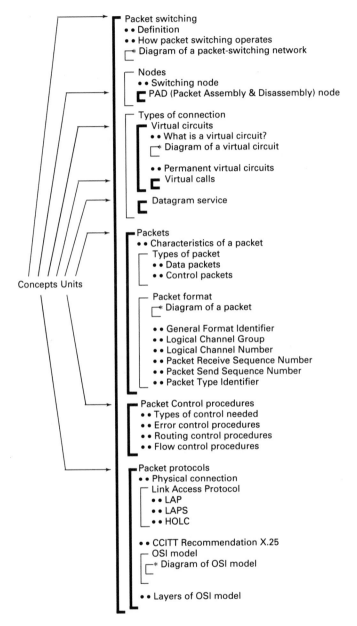

Concepts Units

Packet switching
• • Definition
• • How packet switching operates
└─* Diagram of a packet-switching network

Nodes
• • Switching node
PAD (Packet Assembly & Disassembly) node

Types of connection
Virtual circuits
• • What is a virtual circuit?
└─* Diagram of a virtual circuit

• • Permanent virtual circuits
Virtual calls

Datagram service

Packets
• • Characteristics of a packet
Types of packet
• • Data packets
• • Control packets

Packet format
└─* Diagram of a packet

• • General Format Identifier
• • Logical Channel Group
• • Logical Channel Number
• • Packet Receive Sequence Number
• • Packet Send Sequence Number
• • Packet Type Identifier

Packet Control procedures
• • Types of control needed
• • Error control procedures
• • Routing control procedures
• • Flow control procedures

Packet protocols
• • Physical connection
Link Access Protocol
• • LAP
• • LAPS
• • HOLC

• • CCITT Recommendation X.25
OSI model
└─* Diagram of OSI model

• • Layers of OSI model

Figure 5.3 Concept unit containing description of concept "packet switching."

from its context. It would not be appropriate to have a concept unit labeled "Control Procedures"; it needs to be "Packet Control Procedures."

GLOSSARY

Hyperdocuments ought to have a glossary defining the technical terms used. Any item in the glossary is a candidate for building a concept unit.

The software should *automatically* build buttons for each word in the text which is in the glossary. These buttons link to the glossary entry. The software should also build buttons *automatically* which link to the concept units. The software may check that there is a glossary entry for the subject of each concept unit.

DIFFERENCES BETWEEN BASIC BUILDING BLOCKS AND CONCEPT UNITS

Figure 5.4 summarizes the difference between basic building blocks and concept units. Each concept unit may be the target of hyperlinks in one or more hyperdocuments.

ANALOGY WITH DATA PROCESSING TECHNOLOGY

There are some useful parallels between hypermedia systems and data processing systems. In the early years of data processing, structured techniques were not used. Programmers created spaghetti code. Early attempts at hypertext were also spaghettilike. Spaghetti code and spaghetti hypertext are difficult to modify; maintenance becomes slow, tedious, expensive, and, in some cases, nearly impossible. Use of the structures we have described makes hyperdocuments easy to navigate through and easier to maintain.

In the early years of database technology, designers would gather any collection of fields into database records. Later it became clear that database records ought to be normalized. Normalizing data means that the information about an entity type is stored in the record for that entity type and that no other data is stored in that record. The key of a record uniquely identifies the record. Every attribute in the record "is functionally dependent upon the key, the whole key, and nothing but the key" [2]. Systems with normalized databases have less redundancy and fewer maintenance problems.

The equivalent of data normalization in hyperdocuments is the creation of building blocks containing one idea and one idea only and concept units holding a self-contained set of information about a key concept. Design with these blocks and the structures described in Chapter 3 makes hyperdocuments cleaner for the reader, less redundant, and much easier to maintain.

Basic Building Block	*Concept Unit*
• is the lowest-level envelope.	• may be one building block or may be a hierarchy of envelopes.
• is not usefully subdivisible.	• may be divisible into smaller building blocks and possible lower-level concept units.
• is not necessarily the target of a hyperlink.	• is likely to be the target of multiple hyperlinks, possibly from different documents.
• is not, by itself, worth indexing.	• should be automatically placed in an index of concept units.
	• should have a title which is meaningful when removed from its context.
	• should correspond to an entry in the glossary. Every glossary entry is a potential candidate for a concept unit.
• is drawn with a thin bracket in Fig. 5.3.	• is drawn with a thick bracket in Fig. 5.3.

Figure 5.4   Differences between the basic building block and the concept unit.

After decades of spaghetti design in computing, it became clear that object-oriented design was much better. Object-oriented design identifies object types (entity types) and associates with each object the properties and behavior of that object. In hyperdocuments we should similarly identify the objects and concepts and gather the information about these into a concept *unit*.

Most programmers reinvent things that have been done a thousand times before. To progress faster, we need *reusable design* and building blocks of *reusable code*. The reusable components need to be cataloged so that they are easy to reuse. Similarly in hyperdocuments we need reusable nuggets. There should be an index of concept units, built as automatically as possible, where the concept units are the targets of hyperlinks. Each concept unit can be reused many times and is designed to be as easy to maintain as possible. Many writers may share the same collection of concept units.

6 DIAGRAMS WITH HYPERLINKS

INTRODUCTION   To communicate complex information, diagrams are extremely valuable. An essential part of technical literacy is being able to devise diagrams that make the subject matter as clear as possible.

When I write a textbook chapter, I make notes and create the diagrams before I write any text. The diagrams may go through much modification and polishing before I start on the detailed writing.

USING CHARTS AS   Giving a seminar is quite different from writing a
IN SEMINARS   book. A skilled seminar presenter encapsulates most of his information in charts. The quality of his presentation depends strongly on the quality of his charts. Creating a clear hyperdocument is, in some ways, closer to creating a seminar than to writing a book. Where possible, the information should be summarized and illustrated in charts and diagrams.

Sometimes a chart in a seminar consists of a list of items, each of which the presenter will talk about. In a hyperdocument, each item on such a list may be the title of an envelope which the viewer can open if he wishes. In Chapter 2, for example, we described types of hyperdocuments which are particularly useful. We could have put a summary of these on a chart as shown in Fig. 6.1.

The three dots show that the reader can open these envelopes. This would produce four more detailed charts, shown in Fig. 6.2.

Unlike with a seminar or videotape, the viewer uses his own initiative about whether he examines these envelopes in more detail. Similarly, when looking at a diagram, he should be able to decide whether to explore the items on the diagram in greater depth.

Some types of hyperdocuments which are particularly useful:

. . . LARGE DOCUMENTS

. . . INTELLIGENT DOCUMENTS

. . . COLLECTIONS OF DOCUMENTS

. . . INTERRELATED SETS OF INFORMATION

Figure 6.1

SELF-EXPLANATORY CAPTIONS AND LABELS

A diagram in a hyperdocument may be referred to by multiple, different sections of the hyperdocument. It is a *nugget* of information. The creator of the diagram cannot be sure what the reader will have read before examining the diagram. The diagram must, therefore, be understandable in its own right.

To make this so, the diagram should have an explanatory caption and brief explanatory labels. The author should assume that readers will often look at the diagram without having read the text which points to the diagram. He should ask himself, "Does my diagram caption explain what the diagram is about?

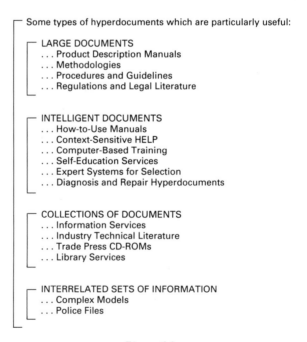

Some types of hyperdocuments which are particularly useful:

LARGE DOCUMENTS
. . . Product Description Manuals
. . . Methodologies
. . . Procedures and Guidelines
. . . Regulations and Legal Literature

INTELLIGENT DOCUMENTS
. . . How-to-Use Manuals
. . . Context-Sensitive HELP
. . . Computer-Based Training
. . . Self-Education Services
. . . Expert Systems for Selection
. . . Diagnosis and Repair Hyperdocuments

COLLECTIONS OF DOCUMENTS
. . . Information Services
. . . Industry Technical Literature
. . . Trade Press CD-ROMs
. . . Library Services

INTERRELATED SETS OF INFORMATION
. . . Complex Models
. . . Police Files

Figure 6.2

Does the caption enable the diagram to be understood without reading the parent text?"

It is strongly recommended that an author devise the diagrams that he will use before he writes the detailed text. He should adjust and polish the diagrams and their labels and captions before writing text.

The leader or manager of a team of authors should examine all the diagrams, preferably before they write much text, to ensure that the diagrams are as clear and appealing as possible and that their labels and captions are fully self-explanatory.

CREATION OF DIAGRAMS

Diagrams in hypertext may be created with tools such as

- A paint program
- An object-oriented draw program
- Software which generates charts from numbers (like that found in many spreadsheet tools)
- A scanner which digitizes diagrams on paper or slides
- A program which allows scanned diagrams to be modified
- A "snap" facility which captures a computer screen—often a screen from some other tool such as a CAD (computer-aided design) or CASE (computer-aided systems engineering) tool

An author should have his own diagramming tools. He may use an assistant who is skilled with paint or draw software.

Diagram Index

Because diagrams are a particularly important aid to understanding subject matter, the hyperdocument user must be able to find the diagrams quickly and easily. They must not be hidden at the end of links which the reader may bypass.

An *index of diagrams* may be compiled automatically by the software. Each index entry will be the heading line for the envelope which contains the diagram. This heading should be written so as to be a useful index entry. It can be independent of the diagram caption. No envelope should contain more than one diagram.

Diagram Envelopes

The reader should be able to find and examine the diagrams independently of the text, as readers of textbooks do. He may find them via the index of diagrams. Often, a more useful way to find them is by having a visible envelope structure, making it clear which envelopes contain diagrams. The dots indicating that a line may be expanded into an envelope may have a different appearance if that envelope contains a diagram (or if it contains a video or sound sequence). The reader may then open the diagram envelopes and look at the diagrams before reading the text.

Figure 6.3 shows the outline of a document structure indicating which envelopes contain diagrams. The hyperdocument software may have a command enabling the reader to open diagram envelopes independently of text.

Figure 6.3   Document structure outline
with diagram envelopes denoted.

ANIMATION AND VIDEO

While the diagrams in most hyperdocuments today are still charts or images, it is useful sometimes to employ moving images. This may be done with animation of computer-generated diagrams, or it may be video (i.e., television segments).

Several of the "draw" software packages provide the capability to provide animation or rapidly changing diagrams. Sometimes these are a rapid succession of separate frames.

Video may be displayed from 12-inch laser disks using conventional television or from CD-ROMs using powerful compression techniques to compress images to a bit rate of from 50K bits per second to 1M bits per second, depending on the amount of movement and the resolution required.

SOUND Opening an envelope or activating a button may cause speech (or other sound) to be played. Good quality speech can be digitized with a bit rate of about 24K bps. Speech may be displayed along with a diagram and, possibly, with a diagram which has some movement or successive highlighting of different parts of the diagram. If an envelope contains speech or video or if a button activates speech or video, the viewer ought to be able to recognize this before initiating the playback.

Increasingly in the future, as technology improves, speech, moving images, and television will become integral parts of hyperdocuments.

WINDOWS When diagrams are used, windows are particularly valuable. It is useful to have the diagram in one window and explanatory text in another. The reader glances back and forth from the text to the diagrams.

The screen of a personal computer may not be of high enough resolution to display diagram and text windows side by side; so, sometimes the viewer has to toggle between the two.

There are two conflicting design objectives. One is to maximize the display area for the figure; the other is to display the figure and text at the same time. The best compromise between these might be to use a relatively small horizontal window for scrolling the text. Various buttons on the diagram might result in the display of temporary pop-on windows containing explanatory text.

BUTTONS ON DIAGRAMS A particularly important characteristic of hyperdocument software is the ability to display buttons which show a part of the diagram and hyperlink from it. The button may be a displayable box surrounding a portion of the diagram. The author creates this box, makes it an appropriate shape and positions it on the diagram. There may be many such boxes on one diagram, each of which has a hyperlink to a different target. The viewer should be able to display the buttons in a rapid sequence, select any button that interests her, and hyperlink from it to explanatory material.

Some hyperdocument software allows the viewer to link to and from diagrams but does not permit areas of the diagram to become buttons. This restriction severely limits the power of the author in using graphics effectively.

Illustration of Buttons on Diagrams

Figure 6.4 shows a diagram of a telephone switching system. The author has placed six buttons on this diagram—the six boxes shown in Fig. 6.5.

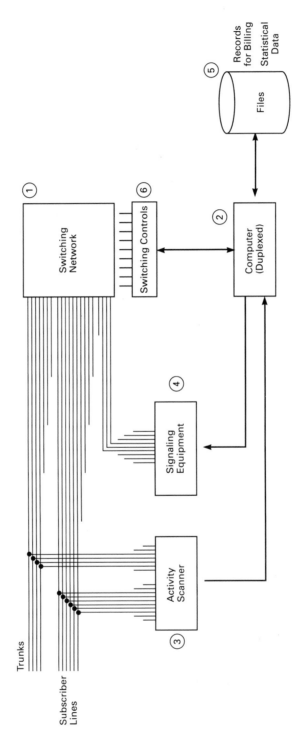

Figure 6.4 Diagram of telephone switching system.

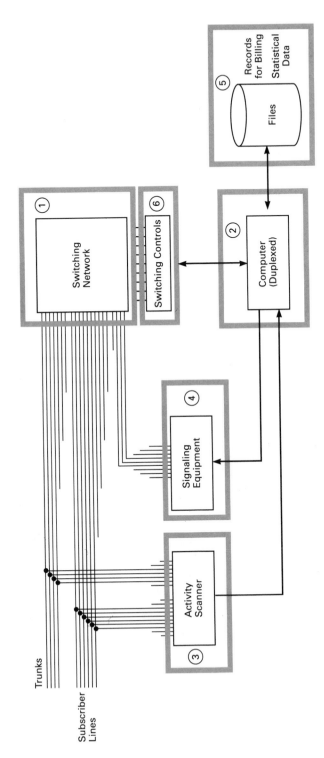

Figure 6.5 Buttons on telephone switching system diagram.

65

There are various signals that must be sent, some to telephones and some to other switching systems. They include "busy" signals, signals to make the telephone ring, dialed numbers, and on-hook/off-hook signals. The signaling equipment generates these signals. The signaling equipment can be regarded as one of the computer output units of this type of system.

Figure 6.6   When a viewer activates the button on "Signaling equipment," shown in Figure 6.5, this explanatory window appears.

One of these six boxes is displayed at a time. The viewer can flip through them very rapidly to see what buttons he can activate. He may select the button shown in Fig. 6.6. This causes the explanation window shown in Fig. 6.6 to be displayed.

Figure 6.7 shows a picture of a skull from a hyperdocument about neurosurgery. The skull can be viewed from the top, side, front, or back, and buttons appear on it. Figure 6.8 shows the result when one of the buttons in Fig. 6.7 is activated.

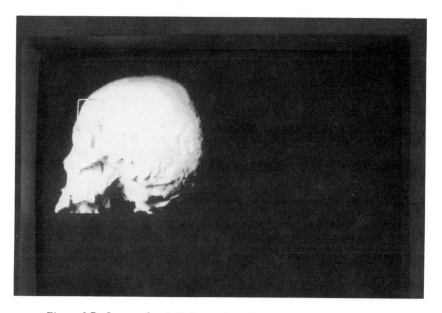

Figure 6.7   Image of a skull from a hyperdocument about neurosurgery.

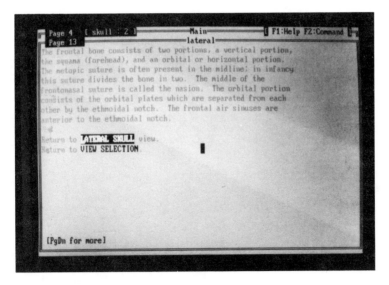

Figure 6.8　Expansion of button referred to in Fig. 6.7.

DIAGRAMS SHOWING THE HYPERDOCUMENT ORGANIZATION

It is often useful to employ a diagram to show the basic organization of a hyperdocument. The reader sees this diagram when (or soon after) he opens the document and can link from it to the different types of material in the document.

Figure 6.9 shows a diagram representing the organization of an article on a software product KBMS. Activating buttons on this diagram takes the viewer into different tutorial segments.

DIAGRAMS SHOULD OCCUPY ONE SCREEN

It is generally desirable that diagrams fit within one screen. If the diagram occupies a larger area than one screen, the viewer should be able to scroll it. However, a diagram that displays too much information tends to be confusing. Usually, it can be broken into separate diagrams of less complexity. Complex diagrams can often be subdivided hierarchically so that there is a simpler "parent" diagram linked to "child" diagrams which show one aspect in more detail.

In writing many textbooks, I have only rarely found the need for a diagram so large that it would have to be scrolled. Sometimes scrolling *is* useful; for example, a picture of the electromagnetic spectrum and its many uses is long and scrollable.

If a diagram does have to be scrolled, it should be designed so that it is scrolled in one dimension, not both. It is usually better to scroll it vertically

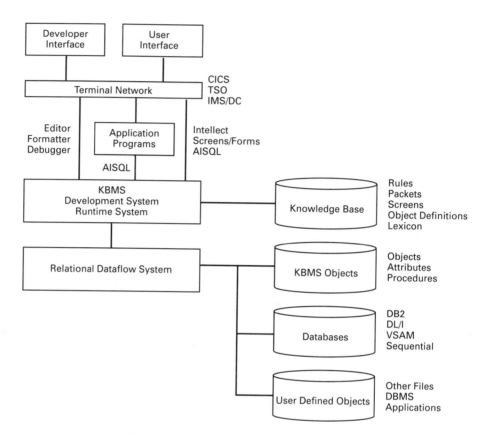

Figure 6.9 Diagram representing the organization of an article on a software product KBMS.

rather than horizontally—for two reasons. First, the viewer scrolls text verti-cally all the time, and the same keys can be used. Second, words written hori-zontally usually fit onto a vertically scrolled diagram better than onto a horizon-tally scrolled diagram. The scrolled diagram should have buttons on it so that the viewer can link to a diagram showing detail which does fit on one screen.

ANIMATION   Some diagrams are natural candidates for animation. Figure 6.10, for example, illustrates time-division switching. A simple, animated version of this could show the circles moving and being switched to the appropriate output channels. A more valuable use of animation would be for illustrating how complex software works (e.g., distrib-uted database software) and how it copes with failures.

Animation generally tends to be useful for illustrating *how things work.*

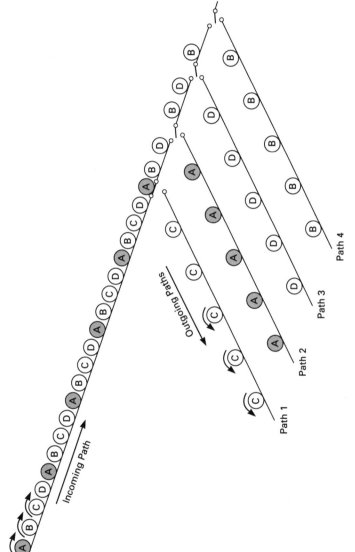

Figure 6.10 Time-division switching.

DIVERSITY

When a lecturer delivers a lengthy seminar with charts all produced by the same charting software, it can become visually tedious. There is a need for diversity, richness, and surprises in the graphics. The same applies to hyperdocuments. Consistency is useful for clarity, but an author should not feel constrained to make every chart look similar. As in news magazines, it is appealing to have a diversity of images. Some may be created with a "draw" or "paint" tool, some with numerical charting software, some with a scanner. Some images may fill the screen, others may be a small part of an envelope with text. The style of the image should be chosen to fit the subject matter as well as possible.

THE NEED FOR HELP IN GRAPHICAL EDITING

Just as some people have an innate ability to write well, so others can communicate well with diagrams. Often, a good writer is poor at diagram design, and a good diagram creator is poor at writing. The creation of good hyperdocuments requires both skill with words *and* skill with diagrams. The words and pictures must support each other to provide maximum ease of communication. Both skills can be learned, but there may not be time to master them both.

Some people have a natural gift for the aesthetics of diagrams and can produce wonderful graphics. It is possible and desirable to teach the principles of competent graphics, but uniquely spectacular graphics defy compositional principles. An artist operates by instinct. As the American painter Ben Shahn once commented, "Aesthetics is for the artist like ornithology is for the birds."

Because of the importance of diagrams in communicating complex ideas, it can pay to have a (human) graphical editor to support authors. Most publishers have a copy editor to clean up the authors' English. A diagram editor can be even more useful in the world of hyperdocuments. Most copy editors lack the ability to be excellent graphical editors.

THE (HUMAN) GRAPHICAL EDITOR

A graphical editor may operate differently from a copy editor. The graphical editor may *create* the diagrams using graphical software. This can save the author time as well as create a more professional product. After some weeks of practice, people using "draw," "paint" and animation software can become very skilled with it. It is necessary to combine this skill with a sense of how to employ diagrams effectively.

The graphical editor needs four skills:

- An understanding of how to communicate well with diagrams
- A sense of graphical aesthetics
- An ability to use explanatory words effectively on diagrams
- The ability to use graphical software with speed and skill

Of these four skills, the sense of aesthetics and understanding of how to communicate well are the most difficult to teach; so a person should be selected who has an innate talent in these areas.

The authors being helped by a graphical editor may create color pencil sketches of diagrams with appropriate labels and explanations. The editor builds the screen versions of these, and the author reviews them. It helps if the author uses the same software as the editor so that she can create a version of what she likes and, when necessary, can adjust the work of the editor.

BOOKS TO READ   I would give any graphical editor two entertaining books to read and tell him to absorb every word in them. David Ogilvy's *Ogilvy on Advertising* [1] and Edward Tufte's *The Visual Display of Quantitative Information* [2] are invaluable.

7 DOCUMENTS WITH EMBEDDED INTELLIGENCE

One of the most interesting differences between hyperdocuments and paper documents is that hyperdocuments can have built-in computing routines. Computing within a hyperdocument is sometimes referred to as *embedded intelligence*.

Embedded intelligence may use the techniques of artificial intelligence— or may use conventional programming.

Programmed routines may be executed

- When a document is opened
- When an envelope is opened
- When a button is activated

Programs may be included inside an envelope; we refer to it as an *intelligent envelope*. All links point to *targets* which are envelopes. An *intelligent link* may execute a programmed routine in order to decide to which envelope to go. The routine may involve a dialog with the document user. Possibly a better way to view this is that the button links to a program code envelope which, in turn, links to information envelopes.

UPDATABLE STORAGE

Some of the most valuable uses of intelligent hyperdocuments require the computer to store information about the user, his problem, or his situation. The document "gets to know its user."

CD-ROMs are valuable delivery media for hyperdocuments. However, because a CD-ROM is read-only, information about the user cannot be stored on it. Therefore, software on the CD-ROM must open a file on a writable disk, where updatable information can be kept.

It would be valuable to keep a small amount of updatable information on the CD itself. This could be done with a WORM (write-once, read-many times) CD. Once something is written on a WORM disk, it cannot be changed; it is like a caveman chipping information into stone tablets. However, the capacity of the WORM disk is so great that every update can be written on a new stone tablet and the old one thrown away. Fifty megabytes of an 800-megabyte WORM disk might be allocated to this throwaway writing.

It would be more elegant to have a CD-ROM, mass-producible at their amazingly low cost, with a small amount of updatable storage. This is sometimes referred to as a CD-PROM, the "P" standing for "programmable." A variety of storage devices and formats may compete to be our future intelligent hypermedia.

Meanwhile, today's CD-ROM can be used, backed up by a writable disk, or the hyperdocuments can reside entirely on magnetic media.

PROGRAMMING AN INTELLIGENT DOCUMENT

The creator of an intelligent document may have to program its intelligence; however, most good writers are not good programmers (and vice versa). Hackers and poets are different breeds. Because of this, it is important to provide useful types of precoded document intelligence and give the writer a friendly mechanism for invoking them.

There are several possibilities:

1. The hyperdocument author writes program code.
2. The author employs an easy-to-use code generator.
3. The author employs an easy-to-use expert-system shell.
4. The author invokes precoded functions.
5. A central service exists to help the author by adding programmed functions to her document.

Perhaps the most common of these options will be the fourth one. This raises an important question: What types of functions should be precoded in hyperdocument authorizing tools? Figure 7.1 lists some types of functions used to embed intelligence into documents and which can be precoded in hyperdocument software.

NAVIGATION AIDS

One of the most important uses of intelligence built into documents is to help the user navigate through the document. A variety of different aids can help the navigation process. These are discussed in Chapter 8.

The user should be able to leave his own marks on the document in the

Aids to user navigation

Facilities for the user to grade envelopes according to how useful they are to him.
Facilities for the user to leave bookmarks, margin notes, etc.
Facilities for varying the visible structure of the document according to user needs.
(see Chapter 8)

Functions for collecting information about the user

The document can request and store details about the reader's needs, problems, skills, or circumstances. The author can use these for making the document adapt its behavior to be as helpful as possible to the user.

Capability for a document to modify its behavior for different users

At many points in the document structure, alternate information may be presented, depending on the user's circumstances. For example, a methodology document may modify the details it gives, depending on the software, machinery, or standards that the user employs.

Facilities for computer-based training

The facilities in authoring tools for computer-based training are built into hyperdocument authoring software.

A simple expert-system shell

The author can build simple rule-based processing into the document. This can be used:
• when the document is opened
• when an envelope is opened
• when a button is activated

Security functions

The document as a whole, or specific envelopes, can be locked. They may possibly be enciphered. They can be unlocked with appropriate authorization codes, passwords, etc. The author is given the ability to build the security features.

Animation

The hyperdocument may present a sequence of images to its viewer, possibly cycling through the sequence. The authoring tool enables the author to build this sequence and make it appear automatically.

Links to other software

• Spreadsheet software
• Executive information systems
• Computer-aided-design software
• CASE tools
• etc.

Figure 7.1   Intelligent hyperdocument functions precoded in authoring tools.

way he might do with a book. He marks the phrases or envelopes that interest him; he leaves "margin" notes; he does the equivalent of turning down the corners of pages or leaving bookmarks. The software should allow him to skip rapidly to his bookmarks and find the notes he has left.

Where there are parts of the document that the user does not want to see, those parts of the document can be rendered invisible either directly by the user or via some intelligence built into the document.

INVISIBLE ENVELOPES

It is useful to have the ability to make the contents of certain envelopes invisible. The following are uses for invisible envelopes:

- **Hiding items the user does not want to see again.** This may lessen user frustration as he navigates through the document.

- **Making the apparent structure of the document simpler.** The document may contain many options and the user needs only one or two of them. The rest might be rendered invisible. For example, a methodology document might be written for multiple products. The user has only one of these products, so the selectable envelopes which relate to other products are made invisible to him.

- **Allowing one CD-ROM to be mastered for multiple publications.** A publisher might want to sell multiple different publications on a CD-ROM, paying for only one master. The buyer should be able to see only the publication for which he has paid, with the rest rendered invisible.

- **Achieving security over segments of the information.** Certain segments of information may be invisible and locked. The user can unlock them with authorization codes if he demonstrates a "need to know." Computer security safeguards, including cryptography, may be applied to such information.

- **Hiding items for print.** The printed version of a document may need to contain items not in the electronic version because the printed version does not have hyperlinks. These may be present in the printed version for editing convenience but are hidden from the viewer of the electronic version.

- **Hiding program code.** Some envelopes in an intelligent document may contain programming for that document. They might contain PROLOG code, for example. A user may feel threatened if suddenly exposed to PROLOG code which he does not understand; therefore, code should be made invisible except to the programmer.

RESTRICTED ACCESS

Security is necessary for military, police, and government material and also for some commercial material. A CD-ROM can be made secure in a way no paper document can. The material on the CD-ROM may be encyphered when high security is needed.

The ability to lock part of a CD-ROM is commercially important. A publisher may want to publish many documents on one CD-ROM, incurring one charge for mastering and distributing it. The customers can read only those documents for which they have paid or those parts of the CD-ROM to which access is free. The CD-ROM may advertise its own contents, encouraging its owner to pay for things he cannot currently access.

Either an entire hyperdocument may be locked or parts of it may be locked. To unlock it, the user may have to enter a password. Passwords are notoriously insecure; so the unlocking may require both a user password and another number such as a departmental authorization code, a vendor's authorization code, a number unique to a machine, a number from an identification card, a number which changes from minute to minute, and is generated by a portable card. Where the number comes from a card, a key, or a machine, it can be a long, unique number, for example, 48 bits, which a human is unlikely to remember or write down.

The hyperdocument may have the capability built into it to request a security code, decode it, and open the relevant parts of the document.

SEARCHING DOCUMENTS

A CD-ROM user may be confronted with a vast body of information. He cannot possibly read all of it. He wants certain information quickly.

The document may have software built into it for enabling the user to search the document by entering search words or combinations of words. Many CD-ROMs have the capability and store indices designed for high-speed searching.

The indices of electronic documents can be more thorough than those in books. They are compiled electronically. They are used at high speed, and word combinations can be used successively to refine the search. Unlike those for a book, the indices on some CD-ROMs occupy ten times the space of the text.

ANALYZING THE USER'S NEEDS

Searching a large document is often unsatisfactory because it can produce no hits or a deluge of hits. Most of the hits may not relate to the user's immediate problem.

To provide more direct help to users, an author (or the management of a team of authors) should ask, "What are the user's problems? What are his needs? What are important issues about the subject matter?" The author provides menu screens relating to these items and the user responds indicating his immediate problems, needs, or issues. The hyperdocument navigation is then based on this knowledge of the user.

This can be done without the document necessarily storing information about its user. The selection of problems or issues may simply result in the display of a table of contents which relates to these problems or issues. The document may contain many alternate tables of contents customized to different needs.

If, however, the hyperdocument stores information about its reader's problems, needs and issues, it can adapt its behavior at different points in its structure. There may be multiple places where it chooses a hierarchy of envelopes to present to the user, based on its knowledge of the user's needs.

To build documents which adapt their behavior in this way, the author does not have to be a programmer. He builds multiple hierarchical overviews of the body of information, customizing these to different sets of users needs. The document contains software for remembering the user needs and selecting relevant overviews.

DOCUMENTS WHICH ADAPT THEIR BEHAVIOR

There are many circumstances in which it is useful to have a document which adapts itself to users' circumstances. The manual of operation for a machine or system may be designed so that it adapts the information it gives depending on the model type, options, or configuration. A machine may have many selectable options and many different models. A system may be configurable in many different ways.

A methodology document may need to be different depending on the user's choice of software or hardware. There may be alternate types of procedures for different circumstances.

The capacity of electronic storage media, especially the CD, is so large that multiple variants of documents can be stored, and the software can select the variant relevant to the users' circumstances.

The front end of a hyperdocument which adapts its presentation to circumstances may be a decision-tree or a rule-based system.

A DECISION-TREE FRONT END

A decision tree is a preplanned procedure which may take the reader through a hierarchy of menus, as illustrated in Fig. 7.2. The menus relate to user needs or problems, different user circumstances, different models of machines, different variations of a system, and so on. Different exit points from this menu dialog link to different sections of one or more hyperdocuments.

A RULE-BASED FRONT END

A rule-based mechanism is different from a decision tree in that it is nonprocedural. Rules can be added to a small rule base at any time, in any sequence. Small rule bases are easy to build with simple software. The rule base makes recommendations to the reader that he examine certain parts of certain documents. He can hyperlink to these, as illustrated in Fig. 7.3.

UNIQUE FORMS OF ADAPTIVE BEHAVIOR

Some documents may adapt their behavior in ways which are unique to the document. For example, a forecast of future technology may be a very complex hyperdocument because there are so many aspects of

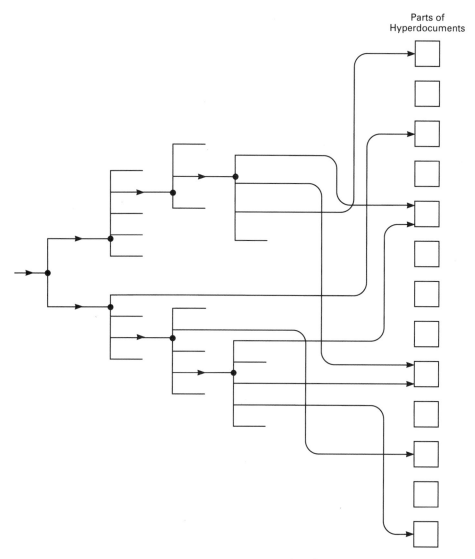

Parts of
Hyperdocuments

Figure 7.2   Decision-tree hierarchy of menus.

technology, most of which will change at a rapid rate over the next 30 years. Each technology is dependent on other technologies. If one technology's impact occurs later than forecast, then other technologies may be delayed also. The hyperdocument might allow the reader to adjust the timing assumptions and observe how a delay or early arrival of one technology causes changes elsewhere.

A system for police specializing in terrorists may store a large body of information about terrorist organizations, individuals, modus operandi, and terror-

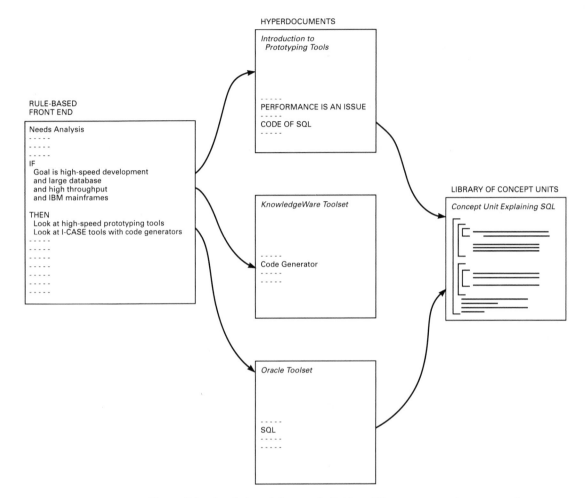

Figure 7.3   A rule-based front end, linking different user needs to parts of documents that relate to those needs.

ist incidents. A threat to blow up a civilian airliner might have characteristics which can be linked in subtle ways to other incidents or suspects. Unique software may exist for correlating characteristics of crimes or threats. The software links to detailed information about possible terrorist methods, individuals, and organizations.

8 HELPING THE USER NAVIGATE

It is not uncommon for users of some existing hypertext products to feel as though they are lost in a forest
of hyperlinks. They drift from one place to another,
activating buttons, often going round in circles. They suspect that there are interesting things hidden in the forest but do not know how to find them. It is
important for the creator of a hyperdocument to pay careful attention to helping
the user find his way around and to locate everything that could be of value to
him.

Being lost among the hyperlinks is often a problem with *one* document—
sometimes with surprisingly small documents if they are ill structured. It is a
larger-scale problem with libraries of documents—for example, a collection of
documents about complex but related products.

Suppose you were a stranger from a Star Trek world in London for one
day and want to see the sights. You have the London tube map (Fig. 8.1). Being a Star Trek character, you do not have to wait for trains; you can hyperlink
instantly to any of the nodes on the map. For each node, you can display a
structured list of the buildings of interest near that location. This is great, but it
would not enable you to find the Crown jewels or Turner's paintings; you don't
know of the existence of the Crown jewels or Turner.

The authorities have created various indices. There is a tourist guide to
London. Using it, you hyperlink to Trafalgar Square and look at Nelson's Col-
umn. Big deal. You hyperlink to Leicester Square and look at the Coliseum.
That was a waste of time; it's not like the one in Rome. You suspect that most
of the things in the tourist guide would be of low interest to you, but you know
that London is one of the richest centers of earthlings' culture. You need some
intelligence in your navigation aids.

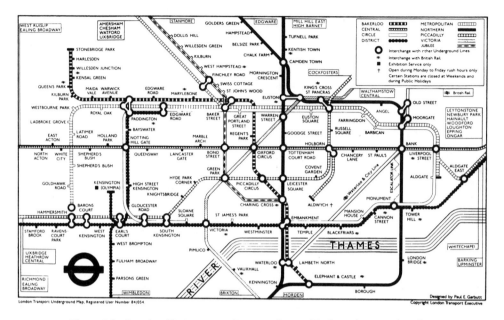

Figure 8.1   London Transport underground map. Each station may be a button in a guide to London. (Courtesy London Transport.)

The computer asks which of the following interests you:

- Culture
- Architecture
- History
- Pubs
- Performing arts
- Sex
- Politics

You indicate culture, and, after another menu, you are given a list of museums:

- British Museum
- Geffrye Museum
- National History Museum
- Museum of London
- Pollock's Toy Museum
- Royal Air Force Museum

- Science Museum
- Victoria and Albert Museum

You hyperlink into the Geffrye Museum. Again, you suspect that there must be additional interesting cultural highlights—but how do you find them? *This, in essence, is the hyperdocument navigation problem.*

WAYS TO MAKE NAVIGATION EFFICIENT

There are many ways to help the user navigate efficiently through hyperdocuments. They are listed in Fig. 8.2. Most important, the document should be well structured, and the structure should be clear to the user.

Features where the computer DOES NOT store information about the user

- The document is WELL-STRUCTURED.
- The structure is based on HIERARCHIES.
- Organizing paradigms other than hierarchies may be used.
- The structure of the document is made CLEARLY VISIBLE.
- The user can navigate through the visible structure AT HIGH SPEED.
- The user can instantly BACKTRACK over the links he traversed.
- The user can instantly return to HOME points if he feels lost.
- The user can have a DIALOG with the system.
- The user can quickly find and look at all the diagrams.

Features where the computer DOES store information about the user

- The system STORES KNOWLEDGE about the user in order to help him.
- The user can MARK the envelopes which interest him.
- The user can make INVISIBLE the envelopes he does not want.
- The user can LEAVE BOOKMARKS at any point in the document.
- The user can LEAVE NOTES at any point in the document.
- The system can use COMPUTER-BASED TRAINING.
- The document ADAPTS its navigation paths to the user's needs.
- The document has a built-in EXPERT SYSTEM.

Figure 8.2　Features that aid hyperdocument navigation.

The document should make the structure visible. The basic structure of any document should be hierarchical, and the user should be able to navigate through the hierarchy very quickly. The bracket diagrams described in Chapters 4 and 5 are probably the best way to achieve this. If documents are not hierarchical in structure, the user can have difficulty understanding the structure and may find that he goes around in loops. There may be many cross-links among hierarchies, links to concept units, and so on. The reader should be able easily to backtrack whenever he follows such links.

The structure will often employ a diagram other than a hierarchical one as a basic scheme for organizing the document. A diagram shows the overall picture in a way which relates to the subject matter. The diagram has buttons on it, and the author hyperlinks from the diagram to explanatory text. Figure 8.3 shows a building-block diagram where each of the building blocks has a button to explanatory text.

In a similar way, a matrix, network diagram, diagram of machinery, or map (such as is shown in the pyramid in Fig. 4.7 and so on) could be the key to the organization of all or part of the document. These diagrams are the top block

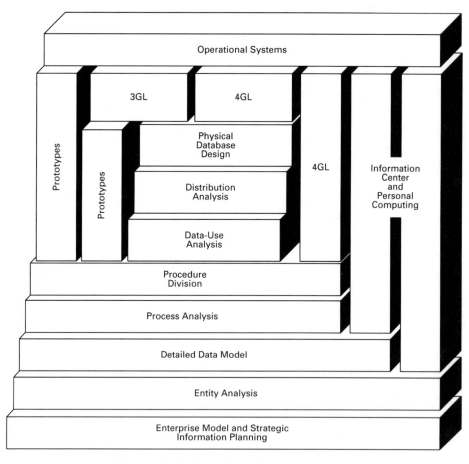

Figure 8.3 Building-block diagram with buttons.

of a hierarchy (or subhierarchy), and they may link to multiple layers lower in the hierarchy. If a viewer feels lost, he should be able to return immediately to the organizing diagram.

BACKTRACKING   When the user follows multiple hyperlinks, he should be able to backtrack immediately if he wishes, reversing over the links he followed. He may use two keys, one which follows hyperlinks and the other which backtracks over links traversed. Better, he should be able to backtrack immediately, using the mouse. Like retracing one's steps with a ball of wool in the Catacombs, the backtrack facility can be activated multiple times until the "home" location is reached. This can be done almost instantaneously with appropriate software (often using a mouse).

The user may close envelopes and return to a higher point in the hierarchy. If he feels lost, he should also be able to return immediately to "home" positions which show the document structure or organizing diagram and allow him to try a different route.

UNDERSTANDING   The first rule for any author is that he should under-
READERS' NEEDS   stand his audience. He must know why they are reading his material and what problems or issues he can help them with. Knowing this, he might state the problems and issues in such a way that the user can identify them and hyperlink to information, tutorials, or action recommendations.

A hyperdocument or library of documents might have a front-end dialog which provides action-oriented solutions to problems and issues. The reader can examine the problem list, select an item from it, and be linked to those parts of the document which deal with that problem.

This valuable type of front-end dialog can be built with a hyperdocument authorizing system, without the author having to be a programmer. The author simply builds appropriate menus and links.

A HIERARCHY OF   Probably the best way of representing user problems,
USER CONCERNS   needs, issues, and questions is with a hierarchy built with brackets so that hierarchical envelopes can be opened and closed at high speed. In other words, the same technique should be used as with the table of contents. It is a good exercise in understanding his readers for *any* author to create such a hierarchy.

A CD-ROM version of the *Engineering Data Compendium* [1], an encyclopedia concerned with the human engineering techniques for complex systems, presents two hierarchical structures to its users. The first is the *table of contents,* in which the nuggets of information are organized hierarchically by subject, as in any well-structured textbook. The second is a *design checklist* combined with a set of *design questions.* These form an application-oriented hierarchical navigation structure related to the users' problems.

The user of a large document is not going to read all of it. Relying only on the table of contents, he might miss items which can solve his problems. A second navigation hierarchy based directly on users' problems, issues, and questions can help him find whatever items are useful to him. Figure 8.4 illustrates two hierarchies for accessing the building blocks. In some cases, it may be useful to have more than two hierarchies for navigation.

INTERDISCIPLINARY BARRIERS

The authors of the *Engineering Data Compendium* found that many designers of complex systems fail to exploit much useful information about human perception and performance *because they do not find it.* The information they need tends to be organized into different disciplines, and there is little communication between separate disciplines. Each discipline has a large volume of information and conventions used to package the research results for the scientific community. Designers need knowledge which should be culled from multiple disciplines. The *Compendium* authors used the term *cross-disciplinary chokepoints* to describe the barriers between disciplines [2]. This is a problem the *Compendium* authors set out to solve.

The same problem applies to many different areas. Hyperdocuments structured like those in Fig. 8.4 can help to solve the problem. Often, it is on a smaller scale than that solved with the *Engineering Data Compendium* CD. Most industries tend to have literature summarizing products, and each product report is usually an isolated document. The potential user of such reports has problems and issues of concern to him and would like to have hyperlinks to the documents that deal with his concerns. A user-oriented index of reports (like *Consumer Guide* reports) should be designed to provide action-oriented solutions to user problems.

WHEN THE COMPUTER STORES INFORMATION ABOUT THE USER

These techniques for good navigation do not require the computer to store any information about the user. When the computer stores information about the user's likes, dislikes, problems, and skills, it can be more helpful. Figure 8.2 is divided into features important for hyperdocument navigation in which the computer *does not* store information about the user and techniques for which the computer *does* store such information.

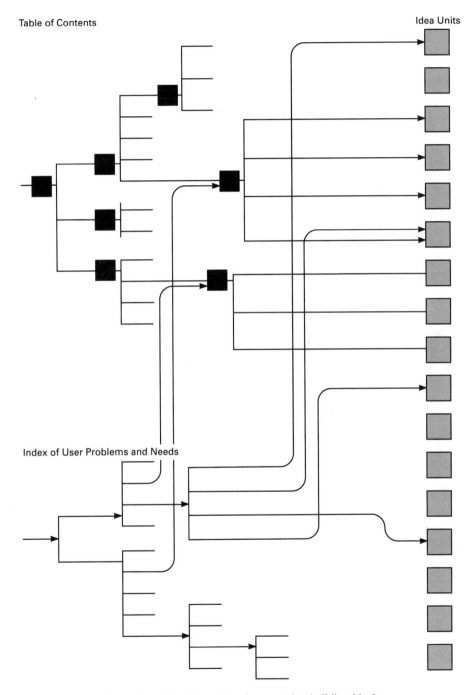

Table of Contents

Idea Units

Index of User Problems and Needs

Figure 8.4   Two hierarchies for accessing building blocks.

KNOWING WHERE YOU HAVE BEEN When exploring a complex hyperdocument, it is useful to know where you have been. When a user signs on, the software may create a record for that user which will track where he goes. This same record may also indicate whether he likes where he has been.

Perhaps the neatest way of showing a user where he has been and what he likes and dislikes is to color the brackets and dots of an envelope diagram. If an envelope diagram is used as the main aid to navigation, the brackets and dots may be white when the user starts.

When the user opens an innermost envelope and stays there long enough to read it (as opposed to scrolling rapidly across it), this bracket could be colored yellow, for instance. When he has visited all of the envelopes in a higher-level bracket, that bracket is colored yellow. He can instantly do a group CLOSE and see (from the colors of the closed-envelope dots) which he has not yet visited.

He may also want to mark the envelopes to indicate the degree to which they are useful to him. He may mark the envelopes as

- Very useful.
- Useful, but I may not revisit it.
- Not useful.
- Useless; get rid of it.

If he indicates that an envelope is in the first category, it may be colored red (a standard color for indicating something important). If it is in the second category, it might be colored orange (or a lighter shade of red). If it is not useful, it is colored blue. If he says "Get rid of it," the bracket is made invisible.

As illustrated in Chapters 4 and 5, brackets can be thick or thin. The reader may make brackets (and their dots) thick to indicate that the envelope is special to him.

BOOKMARKS We like to place bookmarks in a book. The hyperdocument reader should be able to leave the equivalent of bookmarks. He should be able to go to his first bookmark at any time, skip to the next bookmark, and so on, cycling back to the first.

USER NOTES The user should be able to leave his own notes, comments, criticisms, and soon in the hyperdocument. Whenever he opens an envelope where he has left a note, it will be displayed automatically in a special window. He may also be able to place notes at locations where he has positioned bookmarks.

There ought to be a means of seeing which envelopes have readers' notes without having to open the envelope.

EDITOR NOTES

While it is useful for the reader and author to leave notes in a document, it is also valuable for a copy editor or series editor to leave notes for the author via the same mechanism.

A copy editor may make proposed text changes as well as leave notes. A mechanism is needed for this. The editor may duplicate lines in a different color and modify the duplicate. The color makes the change immediately visible to the author.

STORING KNOWLEDGE ABOUT THE READER

Mechanisms for knowing what envelopes the reader has visited, allowing him to color the brackets or make them thick, allowing him to leave bookmarks and notes, require no work on the part of the author—they merely need the appropriate software mechanisms.

The computer can store more interesting reader-specific information to help the reader navigate. The computer might record the reader's likes, dislikes, skills, concerns, and problems and adapt its presentation of the document accordingly. We discussed a front-end dialog in which the hyperdocument identifies problems and issues and links them to action-oriented solutions. This can be done without any programming being built into the document, but, if the computer knows more about the reader, it might modify the dialog to make it more relevant to the reader. The computer might select different menus and associated links, based on who the reader is, what his skill level is, or how he has responded to questions.

COMPUTER-BASED TRAINING

One form of hyperdocument which adapts its behavior to the viewer is computer-based training products.

The author of these products designs a teaching plan and builds it into the product. The product repeatedly tests the student to see what he knows about a certain topic and adapts its behavior accordingly. It may skip topics; it may return to topics previously covered because the student does not yet understand them.

The authoring techniques of computer-based training are also relevant to some other types of communication.

DOCUMENTS THAT ADAPT TO USER NEEDS

Based on the viewer's identification of his needs, hyperdocument software may select what it presents. For example, some documents contain methodologies for accomplishing complex tasks such as machinery maintenance, software development, or systems planning. These methodologies are different, depending on the tools used or the detailed circumstances.

Some car companies have created hyperdocuments to aid in car maintenance. There are many models of cars and their components, and different models need different approaches. The hyperdocument may ask for details of what model is being worked on. It then eliminates all references to other products and models and presents information specific to the one in question.

Information engineering, an approach to building information systems, is growing in popularity, and hyperdocuments have been built describing in complex detail the methodology for doing this. The methodology is heavily dependent on diagrams manipulated on the screen of a CASE (computer-aided systems engineering) tool set. Different users of the methodology have different CASE tools. The hyperdocument should, therefore, present as much of its material as possible in a tool-independent fashion and select other material based on the reader's statement of what tools he is using. Once it knows the reader's tool set, for the rest of the time that person uses the hyperdocument, it will link only to envelopes which contain diagrams from that tool set and techniques relevant to the tool set.

There are many such examples where the hyperdocument should automatically adapt its navigation paths to the circumstances of the reader.

REQUIREMENTS IN THE SOFTWARE

Most of the navigation aids discussed in this chapter require features in the hyperdocument software. This is a particularly important aspect of the software because ease of navigation is so important in hypermedia. Figure 8.5 lists software features required to help the users navigate.

Essential features

The software should:

- encourage well-structured organization of the document.

- make the structure of the document CLEARLY VISIBLE to the reader.
  Graphics are essential for this.

- enable the user to navigate through the visible structure AT HIGH SPEED.

- enable the user to instantly BACKTRACK over the links he traversed.

- enable the user to instantly return to HOME points if he feels lost.

- enable the user to build buttons on diagrams.

- enable the user to quickly find and look at all diagrams.

Features that enable the user to mark up the document

The software should:

- enable the user to MARK the envelopes which interest him, e.g., with color codes.

- enable the user to MAKE INVISIBLE the envelopes he does not want.

- enable the user to LEAVE BOOKMARKS at any point in the document.

- enable the user to LEAVE NOTES at any point in the document.

More specialized features

The software should:

- STORE KNOWLEDGE about the user's skills and circumstances in order to help him.

- enable the author to create a document which ADAPTS its navigation paths to the user's circumstances.

- provide COMPUTER-BASED TRAINING facilities.

- provide EXPERT-SYSTEM facilities to aid in navigation.

Figure 8.5 Features required in hyperdocument software to build the maximum ease of navigation.

PART III GUIDELINES FOR AUTHORS

9 THE PROCESS OF HYPERDOCUMENT CREATION

This section of the book gives guidelines to authors about how to write good hyperdocuments. Much of the advice would be equally valid for authors of paper documents or books. If authors of paper documents structured their work clearly into building blocks, concepts units, and charts, and followed the advice of this book, they would usually create documents of greater value to their readers.

Software for creating hyperdocuments can be a great help to authors of paper documents.

THE PRIMARY GOAL

It is the job of the author of the hyperdocument to communicate information in such a way as to make it as valuable as possible to the reader. Any other goal is subordinate to this.

It is not the primary goal of the author to be original or intellectual. Some authors subconsciously write advertisements for themselves. They want to demonstrate their brilliance or intellect. Some books written by professors are intellectual but valueless. The attempt to demonstrate intellect usually results in loss of clarity.

To create value for the reader the hyperdocument must have maximum clarity and, like a smoothly oiled machine, must help the reader to navigate to the items which help him.

Maximum clarity requires

- Clear structuring (Chapters 4 to 6)
- Clear organization of ideas (Chapter 10)
- Clear English (Chapter 11)

- Clear diagrams (Chapters 12 to 14)
- Clear navigation (Chapters 7 and 8)

It is to be hoped that your hyperdocument can be creative, original, and brilliant, but remember that your overriding goal is to help the reader to make your hyperdocument as valuable as possible.

ORIGINALITY

Some authors strive for "originality." Originality for its own sake cuts across the primary objective of helping the reader. Rosser Reeves, in his classic book on advertising wrote, "What do you want out of me? Fine writing? Do you want masterpieces? Do you want glowing things that can be framed by copywriters? *Or do you want to see the goddamned sales curve start moving up?"* [1] He comments, "Preoccupied with originality, copywriters pursue something as illusory as swamp fire, for which the Latin phrase is *Ignis factuus."*

Mozart said, "I have never made the slightest attempt to compose anything original." Like Mozart, you should explore the frontiers of the tools at your disposal. Find out what new things you can do with your software. Experiment with the images that can fill a screen. Try to create effects that are beautiful or captivating. Explore the ways to use intelligent envelopes, hyperlinks or expert systems — but put the results of such experiments into your hyperdocument *only* if they improve its value to the reader.

The exploration of new forms applies mainly to the use of diagrams, structures, and programs rather than to the use of English. The use of English should be classical and straightforward. English usage has been refined for centuries by millions of writers and their results distilled in style guides which you are unlikely to improve upon. Deviate from these at your peril. The use of hyperlinks, computer artwork, and intelligent envelopes is new and evolving daily. Humankind's hyperdocument masterpieces have yet to be created.

CRAFTSMANSHIP IN THE DETAILS

The author who wants to create an excellent hyperdocument should pay attention to the details. Use interesting illustrations. Employ an artist who can make the artwork beautiful. Search for the perfect metaphor. Refine the structure repeatedly. Polish the English. Mies Van Der Rohe said of architecture, "God is in the details."

CD-ROMS may be too large to have everything painstakingly polished. It may be appropriate to have a nucleus which is elegant and beautifully thought out, with hyperlinks to large amounts of detail or reference material which is unpolished but well indexed.

THINKING ABOUT THE READER

It is worth repeating that the first rule for any communicator is to understand her audience. The author should think carefully about who will use the hyperdocument:

- Who are the readers?
- Why are they reading the hyperdocument?
- What do they already know?
- What technical words do they understand?
- What are their problems, needs and issues?
- How can the author help them?
- What constitutes value for the reader when he uses the hyperdocument?
- How can this value be maximized?

Some authors do not start by thinking about the reader; they write in order to see their own words. This is intellectual masturbation. Writing is a process of communicating with other people, and, to do that well, you must understand those people. Try to put yourself in their heads and view your writing from their perspectives.

Some of the nuggets of a hyperdocument may be timeless tutorials not tailored to any specific reader. These are the concept units—subdocuments which can be read independently of context. They can be centrally indexed and hyperlinked into many documents. They need to be simple, elegant, and tutorially clear.

Other parts of a hyperdocument may be reader-specific, that is, related to the reader's knowledge or to his problems or circumstances.

Some hyperdocuments, then, are a mix of reader-independent concept units, which are firm and unchanging, and more fluid reader-specific material, which addresses the readers' needs and which links to the concept units where appropriate.

As we described in Chapter 8, the author may build different ways of navigating through the hyperdocument to meet the needs of different readers.

SEARCH FOR VISUAL FORMS OF REPRESENTATION

To a large extent, hyperdocuments are a visual medium. The author should develop skills with visual presentation as well as skill with words. (See Chapters 12, 13, and 14.)

Good textbooks have many diagrams. A hyperdocument should be more visual in its representation than a textbook. The author should examine the subject matter and decide how he can effectively use diagrams, lists, and hierarchies. He should say to himself, "If I were presenting this as a lecture, what charts could I use?" Those charts should be in the hyperdocument.

When he finds himself writing long sequences of text, he should ask, "Can I represent some of the ideas as a bullet list or a chart? Would menus help? Would a decision tree help?" The author should constantly *categorize* and *make the categorization visual*. Hyperdocuments on most subjects should not have more than 200 lines of contiguous text (in multiple envelopes) without a bullet list, chart, diagram, or summary.

As commented upon earlier, creating a good hyperdocument is in some ways closer to creating a seminar than to writing a book. The author breaks the information into nuggets and determines how a computer can present the nuggets so that they communicate as effectively as possible. A chart is often the best way of presenting a nugget of information.

More than any other writer, advertising copywriters are trained to present nuggets of information. Advertisements live or die depending on how well they communicate. Hyperdocument creators should study advertisements and how their authors use English, their headlines, their copy, their layout, and their graphics. Excellent books exist on the techniques of advertising. The skill of the advertising copywriter is in using concise words, and good typography, layout, and images may be emulated, while "hype," sensationalism, and attention-getting devices should be avoided.

DEVELOPMENT PROCEDURE

The procedure for creating a hyperdocument should be planned before work begins. It should include the steps in Fig. 9.1. Figure 9.2 expands some of the preparation part of Fig. 9.1.

It is important that a hyperdocument should be extensively reviewed and field-tested and improved as a result of this feedback. The planning of who will review and field-test the document should be done during the preparation phase.

Preparation

. . . Determine who will read the document.
. . . Determine the goals of the document.
. . . Determine who will create the document.
. . . Determine what resources will be used to help the author(s).
. . . Determine what media and standards will be used.
. . . Determine what subject items should be in the document.

Creation

. . . Design the document.
. . . Author the document.
. . . Review and improve the document.
. . . Field test and polish the document.
. . . Establish the procedure for ongoing updating.

Figure 9.1   Creating a hyperdocument.

Preparation
. . . Determine who will read the document.
─ Determine the goals of the document.
   . . . Determine overall goals.
   . . . Determine who the readers will be.
   . . . List reader problems, needs, and issues which should be addressed.
   . . . List ways in which the document can be valuable to its readers.
   . . . Prioritize the types of value.

. . . Determine who will create the document.
─ Determine what resources will be used to help the author(s).
   ─ Software resources
      • Hyperdocument authoring software
      • "Paint" and "Draw" software
      • Animation software
      • Numeric charting software
      • Word-processing software
      • Spelling checker
      • Grammar checker
      • Electronic publishing software
      • CD-ROM software
      • Software for video media
      • Other software for intelligent documents

   ─ Human resources
      • Copy editor
      • Graphics artist (skilled with diagramming and animation software)
      • Scanning service
      • Hyperdocument coordinator (discussed in Chapter 16)
      • Reviewers
      • Subject matter experts

   ─ Information resources
      • Central glossary
      • Central collection of acronyms
      • Central collection of concept units
      • Central collection of diagrams
      • Document templates

─ Determine what media and standards will be used.
   . . . Establish what personal computer facilities the reader will use.
   . . . Establish the graphics standards.
   . . . Establish what external video devices will be used, if any.
   . . . Establish the display guidelines.
   . . . Establish the typography guidelines.

─ Determine what subject items should be in the document.
   . . . Brainstorm what items should be in the document.
   . . . Determine how the document can attack user problems, needs, and issues.
   . . . Create an initial document structure.
   . . . Review the proposed content and structure with potential users.
   . . . Brainstorm possible improvements in the structure.

. . . Determine who will review and field test the document.

Figure 9.2 Preparation prior to authoring a hyperdocument.

10 ORGANIZING ONE'S THOUGHTS

IDEA PROCESSORS A particularly valuable part of the hypermedia toolkit are facilities that enable an author to organize his thoughts. Elegantly structured documents are not created in a single flash of inspiration. The author has many ideas at different times. He needs to record these ideas and progressively maneuver them into structures which are as clear as possible. The toolkit should help him have ideas and arrange them into valuable patterns. Good hyperdocuments are like fine brandy: their ideas and their structure are refined many times. Conceptual clarity comes slowly.

Software which enables an author to organize his ideas is referred to as an "outliner," "idea processor," or "thought processor." We shall use the term *idea processor*.

An idea processor should enable an author to jot down ideas as they occur to him and arrange them into structures. It should enable him to shuffle the ideas quickly, group them, link them, prioritize them, arrange them into hierarchies or networks, test them, juxtapose the ideas to suggest new ideas, and select the ideas which work best. The easier this is to do, the more valuable is the idea processor. An author often types thoughts in a stream of consciousness. He must organize them into useful structures.

An author does this idea processing:

- **at the earliest stages of creating a document, before he writes anything:** The more he explores and organizes ideas before he writes, the better the document is likely to be.

- **while he is writing:** The process of writing triggers many new ideas. He should be able to flip instantly from his word processor or graphics tool to his pool of ideas when thoughts strike him.

- **when he is polishing his work:** Much reshuffling is likely to occur when polishing a hyperdocument. The more thorough the criticism and polishing, the better the final document.

Idea processors are valuable for conventional writing. They are, perhaps, even more important when creating hyperdocuments because hyperdocuments are so fluid and susceptible to multiple arrangements. New ideas can be added to hyperdocuments quickly.

The tool which enables the author to shuffle ideas and arrange them into structures should be the same tool which enables him to shuffle nuggets of the document itself and arrange them into structures.

We have stressed that your first task as an author is to think about your readers. As you do this, jot down all the ideas that might be useful to your audience. As you write, many more ideas will occur to you. Write all these down, and then use software which helps organize the random ideas into the most useful structures.

NOTE CARDS

When writing essays or papers, students are sometimes taught to write their ideas on note cards. They can lay out the note cards on the desk and arrange them in different ways. As they associate ideas, they can clip them together with paper clips. An idea processor should provide the equivalent of note cards. The author has many ideas jotted down in brief note form, sometimes with references (which he abbreviates to a few letters) and page numbers. He should be able to scroll through these ideas very rapidly and group them together. He may group ideas into brackets:

```
⎡  Idea 2
⎢  Idea 37
⎢  Idea 18
⎣  Idea 46
```

He can rapidly scroll through the brackets and rearrange them.

ENVELOPES

A single idea may be on one line or multiple lines. If it is on multiple lines, he should be able to shrink it to one line by contracting an envelope. The author should be able to put a collection of ideas into an envelope—drawn with a bracket—and shrink that envelope to one line.

He may want to take an idea and write some text as interesting phrases occur to him. He might want to sketch a diagram roughly. He "fleshes out" the idea. This material should reside in an envelope that he can open or close at the touch of a mouse button.

He is then able to scroll and shuffle lines on the screen, where each line might be a one-line idea or a contracted envelope containing a multiline idea, a piece of text, a picture, an animated picture or a program. Again, he can group these one-liners into brackets:

```
Idea 2
 . . Idea 37
 . . Idea 18 with fragments of text
Idea 42
 . . Idea 48: a diagram
 . . Idea 5: text
```

HIERARCHIES

As he groups ideas into envelopes, he may want to put envelopes inside envelopes. He may expand an idea into subcomponents, creating a hierarchy. Hierarchies can be contracted to one line so that they can be shuffled with the other ideas. In this way, the author may steadily accumulate larger building blocks:

```
Idea 2
 . . Idea 37
 . . Idea 18 with fragments of text
 . . . Idea 42, a hierarchy of other ideas
 . . Idea 61, a list of other ideas
Idea 3
 . . . Idea 5: text constructed hierarchically
 . . . Idea 48: a hierarchy of text and diagrams
```

As before, two dots at the start of a line indicate that the line is an envelope that can be opened. Three dots at the start of a line indicate that the envelope contains other envelopes.

The author may open up any of the preceding envelopes; for example, here he opens up Idea 42:

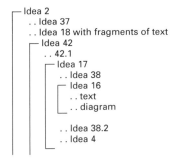

```
Idea 2
 . . Idea 37
 . . Idea 18 with fragments of text
Idea 42
 . . 42.1
Idea 17
 . . Idea 38
Idea 16
 . . text
 . . diagram

 . . Idea 38.2
 . . Idea 4
```

```
    ┌
    │  ┌ Idea 13
    │  │ Idea 72
    │  │
    │  └
    │  . . Idea 61, a list of other ideas
    │  Idea 3
    │  . . . Idea 5: text constructed hierarchically
    └  . . . Idea 48: a hierarchy of text and diagrams
```

TOP-DOWN AND BOTTOM-UP THINKING

In creating documents, we do two types of design. First, we take ideas about details and link them together into structures. This is called *bottom-up design*. Second, we take high-level ideas and decompose them into detail. This is called *top-down design*.

Idea-processor software should enable an author to do both bottom-up and top-down thinking the instant ideas strike him. As he decomposes ideas into detail he should be able to move ideas from elsewhere in his collection into the structure. The mixture of top-down and bottom-up thinking goes on throughout the authoring process.

TABLE OF CONTENTS

Early in the process of thinking about a document an author should list its table of contents. The table of contents may be subdivided hierarchically:

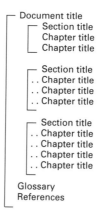

```
    ┌ Document title
    │  ┌ Section title
    │  │ Chapter title
    │  └ Chapter title
    │
    │  ┌ Section title
    │  │ . . Chapter title
    │  │ . . Chapter title
    │  └ . . Chapter title
    │
    │  ┌ Section title
    │  │ . . Chapter title
    │  │ . . Chapter title
    │  │ . . Chapter title
    │  └ . . Chapter title
    │
    │ Glossary
    └ References
```

The table of contents will change steadily as the author's ideas evolve. As an author writes chapters he finds the need to split them, combine them, or change their titles. Even after the first version of the document is complete, the process of criticism and polishing may cause the contents to be reorganized.

There is likely to be more such reorganization with a hyperdocument than with a paper document. The authoring tools need to be designed for this flexibility of reorganization, which means that they must be able to rebuild hyperlinks automatically when the author shuffles the contents (as described in "Maintenance," Chapter 15).

The author should build his table of contents independently of his collection of ideas. He should make each chapter an envelope. He should then go through the collection of ideas allocating them to chapters, and putting them into the chapter envelopes. He will probably find that some of the ideas do not fit the table of contents, so he may want to change the table of contents to incorporate them. He will find that some chapters have little in them, so he will direct his thoughts to useful source material for those chapters.

Before he starts allocating ideas to chapters he may want to think about each chapter and decide what would be a useful structure for it. What subjects should it contain?

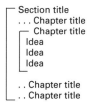

He then allocates the ideas to this structure.

The processes of bottom-up and top-down thinking are intertwined. Both top-down and bottom-up ideas are likely to occur at any instant, and the author should be able to add them to the evolving structure. The structure will continue to evolve throughout the entire period of document creation.

CONCEPT UNITS   Some of the chapters and some of the ideas will relate to *concept units*, as described in Chapter 5. The concept unit should be independent of the chapter layout although it may be heavily referenced by one particular chapter. An entire chapter may be a concept unit. The concept unit needs to be independent of the structure, because it is linked to and from many different places, and possibly from many different documents. There should be a central collection of concept units with an index, as well as a central glossary. The software should be links *automatically* to the glossary and concept units.

As the author's ideas progress new items will emerge that ought to be glossary entries or concept units. He should have an envelope into which he can throw these items prior to the detailed work of building them. In some organizations it is desirable to discuss glossary entries and concept units with a central administrator or editor before they are built, because many authors may use them.

SORTING IDEAS

One of the most useful features of idea processors is the help they give in sorting and categorizing ideas. The author generates an unruly collection of ideas in whatever sequence they occur. He needs to sift through this collection and group the ideas together.

He can do this by setting up brackets (envelopes) and throwing the ideas into the brackets like a mail sorter putting mail into pigeonholes. The brackets may have titles or they may have no title to begin with. As the sorting process continues, the author may create brackets within brackets, building hierarchies of ideas.

Each idea is one line, maybe a line which is a contracted envelope or hierarchy. The author can select the lines one at a time and move them to a bracket. He may select and highlight a particular bracket and then use a "GATHER" function, which moves every line he points to into the selected bracket. In this way, he can sort the ideas very rapidly.

BRAINSTORMING

A fertile way to generate ideas is *brainstorming*. In a brainstorming session, a group of people sit down to discuss ideas relating to given sets of problems or issues, or to discuss ideas about a particular subject. A rule in a brainstorming session is that nobody may be criticized for an idea he has, even if it is wild, impractical or cuckoo. Wild thoughts usually trigger other thoughts, some of which might be useful.

An author at a brainstorming session may be rapidly entering the ideas into a computer, prodding the participants, expanding their ideas, exploring, inventing, and suggesting new directions for the conversation. Sometimes this is done with a group; sometimes it is a two-person interaction. The author may approach or telephone people one after another for brainstorming conversation. After doing this he has an unruly mess of ideas in his computer and sets about cleaning them up, developing the good ideas, culling out the bad ones, removing redundancy, and improving the words used. He needs an idea processor which enables him to sort and relate ideas rapidly, linking them into categories and hierarchies.

PRIORITIZING

Some of the ideas are great, certain to be used in the document; some are not so good; others are dodos. The author does not want to throw out the poor ideas because they might trigger other thoughts, but he would like to rank the ideas, perhaps sorting them by quality.

He may do this by setting up envelopes for ideas of different priorities, for example, "great," "good," "OK," "poor," and "you've got to be kidding." He throws the ideas into these different envelopes like a farmer sorting apples by quality into different tubs. Later, when building chapters, he will look at the high-quality ideas first.

Another, perhaps more valuable, way to categorize ideas is to use color. The software may enable the author to color the lines at the press of a key. He may leave the best ideas white, color the next best ones red, the next yellow, and so on, working down through the spectrum.

MOVING VERSUS COPYING

When the author sifts his collection of ideas, sometimes he wants to *move* an idea line to a different place; sometimes he wants to *copy* the idea line. He may have developed a structure of ideas which he wants to preserve for the time being independently of the allocation of ideas to the table of contents. He may have alternate structures which make sense in different ways.

The commands for sifting ideas, then, should work in two modes: MOVE and COPY.

When he uses a GATHER command, gathering ideas into a selected bracket, the author should be able to use a GATHER MOVE, in which case each chosen line moves to the bracket, or a GATHER COPY, in which case the chosen lines are copied.

A COPY command should be able to clone a whole envelope or hierarchy of envelopes.

WINDOWS

It is useful to have two or more windows when processing ideas. This helps an author to think about how one idea in a large collection of ideas might relate to other ideas. One window may contain a bracket or hierarchy. It might contain part of the table of contents. The other window contains the collection of ideas in such a way that they can be scrolled. The author can scroll steadily through the collection deciding whether to move or link them to what is in the other windows.

EXPERIMENTING WITH DOCUMENT STRUCTURES

For most documents there are many possible structures, and it is not clear at first which will work best. The author should be able to try out alternate possibilities, adjust them, tune them, and compare them. This empirical thinking should go on before the author writes much. However, most authors' ideas mature and change as they are writing and working out detail. They should be able to examine alternate structures as the document evolves.

It is useful for the author to preserve structures of ideas and have the ability to reformat this collection into alternative document structures. He should be able to COPY ideas and hierarchies of ideas into his experimental document structures.

TRIGGERING NEW THOUGHT PATTERNS

New thought patterns often arise from new juxtapositions of ideas. New ideas often occur at the boundaries of existing ideas. The ability to juxtapose ideas in scrollable windows often triggers new ideas.

As the author examines his possible structures, he needs to be able to view them in different ways. He may display the document's breadth, looking at the overall structure with only two levels visible, or he may look at part of it in depth expanding all the envelopes except the lowest. He may expand two chapters in depth, comparing them side by side in windows. He needs the ability to manipulate envelope diagrams very rapidly and compare alternate structures. The capability to examine different views of the document rapidly and clearly is important in attempting to achieve the best possible document structure.

REPLACEMENT OF WORDS

An author often polishes his use of technical words as his document evolves. He may have used different words for the same concept and so may need to modify some of them to achieve uniformity. He may decide to change one word to a better word throughout the document.

The software should give him the capability to search for a given word and, if he wishes, replace that word with a different word *everywhere* it occurs. This may be important when the software automatically builds hyperlinks to glossary items and concept units.

SUBDIVISION OF LISTS OF MORE THAN SEVEN ITEMS

When using lists of items on charts, it is generally a good idea to have not more than seven items. If there are more than seven, the author should examine the list to see whether it can be split. It may simply be divided into two lists, or more, or it may be arranged into subcategories.

It is rare to see lists on television of more than seven items. When lecturers use slides, lists of more than seven items are tedious. Humans listening to lectures, communicating with other people, or interacting with computers employ a part of their memory which can retain information for a short time. Psychologists have described this as a *short-term* memory and have measured its capacity. In complex problem solving, or complex activity at a computer screen, the short-term memory is heavily filled. The complexity of problems that can be solved in the head is related to the quality and form of information that can be held in short-term memory.

The short-term memory cannot hold many items. Experimental measurements conclude that we can remember about seven separate items [1]. This varies by plus or minus two for normal people in different situations. Our short-term memory is constantly in danger of losing its contents due to new inputs or mind-wandering.

In hyperdocuments, it is good practice to avoid, where possible, putting more than seven choices on the screen, or using lists of more than seven items without subdivision. Usually, lists of more than seven items can be divided with subheadings. Like all such guidelines there will occasionally be a good reason to violate it.

The list of useful types of hyperdocuments in Chapter 2 was originally a list with 16 items shown in Fig. 10.1. It was, therefore, divided into subcategories as shown in Fig. 10.2.

The author should take all such lists with more than seven items and see whether he can meaningfully categorize them, adding a hierarchical grouping.

Bracket diagram editors are useful for this. A list can be grouped into two or more brackets, adding another level to a hierarchy. It is good mental discipline to always try to do this with long lists. Usually, it causes the author to shuffle the list into new categories which are useful to the reader.

Perhaps this human capacity to cope with seven items explains why the number *seven* is found so frequently in ancient literature and religion (although mystic literature has far more complex explanations!) We have Seven Wonders of the World, seven deadly sins, the seven seas, the Seven Sages, the Seven Hills of Rome, the seven daughters of Atlas, the seven fat years followed by seven lean years, the Seven Pillars of Wisdom, and even Snow White had Seven Dwarfs.

```
┌─ List of Valuable Hyperdocument Applications
│  . . Product description manuals
│  . . Methodologies
│  . . Procedures and guidelines
│  . . Regulations and legal literature
│  . . How-to-use manuals
│  . . Context-sensitive HELP
│  . . Computer-based training
│  . . Self-education services
│  . . Expert systems for selection
│  . . Diagnosis and repair hyperdocuments
│  . . Information services
│  . . Industry technical literature
│  . . Trade press CD-ROMs
│  . . Library services
│  . . Complex models
└─ . . Police files
```

Figure 10.1   List of Valuable Hyperdocument Applications.

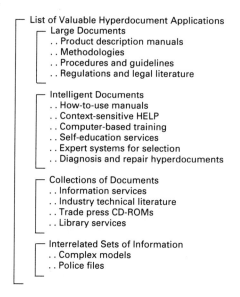

Figure 10.2   List shown in Fig 10.1, divided into subcategories.

ASSOCIATING TWO LISTS   Sometimes an author needs to associate items in separate lists. He might have a list of goals, for example, and a list of products which could help to meet different goals. He might have a list of messages which he wants to communicate and a list of anecdotes which illustrate the messages. He might have a list of issues and a list of possible actions.

To associate the lists he may take the items on the most important list (the one which is closer to the content structure of the document). Let us call this the **X** list. He creates an envelope (bracket) for each item on the **X** list. He then examines the other list, the **Y** list, and allocates **Y** items to the **X** brackets. He may put multiple **Y** items into each bracket. To help do this he might scroll the **Y** list in one window by the **X** brackets in an adjacent window, picking the items to go into each bracket.

The resulting hyperdocument might display the **X** items on a screen, allowing the viewer to select any one of them. When the viewer selects an **X** item, the appropriate **Y** items are displayed. When he selects a different **X,** a different **Y** set are displayed which might have considerable overlap with the first **Y** set.

For example, the viewer might select a problem which is of concern to him and the computer opens an envelope showing products which would help to solve that problem. The viewer selects a different problem and the computer opens a different envelope of products which has some overlap with the first.

EVALUATING THE STRUCTURE

The author should acquire the mental habit of asking certain questions about envelopes as he builds them. Every envelope other than the lowest should be expanded to one level so that a list is displayed of its subenvelopes, and the following questions should be asked:

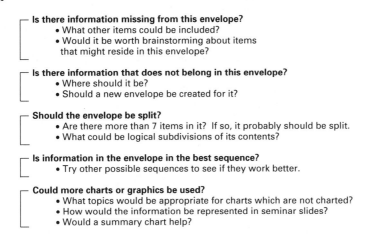

Is there information missing from this envelope?
- What other items could be included?
- Would it be worth brainstorming about items that might reside in this envelope?

Is there information that does not belong in this envelope?
- Where should it be?
- Should a new envelope be created for it?

Should the envelope be split?
- Are there more than 7 items in it? If so, it probably should be split.
- What could be logical subdivisions of its contents?

Is information in the envelope in the best sequence?
- Try other possible sequences to see if they work better.

Could more charts or graphics be used?
- What topics would be appropriate for charts which are not charted?
- How would the information be represented in seminar slides?
- Would a summary chart help?

These questions should be asked (quickly) about all envelopes other than the lowest. They are particularly important to ask about concept units, chapters, and high-level building blocks, and about the document as a whole.

BUILDING A STRUCTURE AROUND EXISTING TEXT

Sometimes an author uses existing text not in hyperdocument format. He may read an ASCII file or word-processed file or scan a document into his hyperdocument authoring software.

The software should allow him to build brackets very quickly around existing text. He may highlight a piece of text and instruct the system to create a bracket around it. He can give titles to such brackets where they do not exist in the original and quickly build a hierarchy which allows fast navigation.

Existing text may then be interleaved with the author's idea processing and empirical hyperdocument structuring.

CHAPTER AND FIGURE NUMBERS

An author should not allocate sequential chapter numbers until close to the end of his work. He is likely to modify his table of contents often as his ideas evolve. If the chapters were numbered sequentially, he would have to constantly change the chapter numbers. This can be a problem because each chapter may make references to other chapters, and these references change.

Instead of using numbers, an author might allocate letters for the chapters, intending to switch them to numbers later. A useful technique is to start each chapter number with an exclamation mark: !3, !21 or !D, !BC. A character string starting with "!" will not appear in the text for other purposes. When the author wants to change chapter numbers he can instruct the authoring software to change this unique character string everywhere it occurs.

The same concern applies to figure numbers. These might have a prefix which is the number of the chapter they appear in. The author might number the figures for Chapter 5 as !5.1, !5.2, and so on. He can then instruct the computer to change a figure number in every place where it occurs.

The final numbering of the chapters, envelopes, and figures might be done automatically by the hyperdocument authoring software.

11 CLARITY IN THE USE OF ENGLISH

SHORT BLOCKS OF TEXT   It is tedious to read lengthy tracts of English on the screen of a computer. Hyperdocuments should be highly structured and consist of relatively short blocks of English. It is a useful working rule that one envelope should contain no more than 100 lines of English. The size of most envelopes should be less than 50 lines (and less than three screens). Like the guideline about lists not exceeding seven items without subdivision, this rule will sometimes be broken, but usually an envelope of more than 100 lines is either unnecessary verbiage or else can be subdivided into separate ideas. No block of text in this book exceeds 100 lines. In all the textbooks I have written, almost no block of text exceeds 100 lines, and, if it does, it should have been subdivided.

SHORT SENTENCES   Textbooks and hyperdocuments sometimes deal with difficult ideas. It is the task of the author to make those ideas as easy to grasp as possible. The text should be clear and smoothly "oiled." The author increases the difficulty for the reader if he uses long, convoluted sentences. His sentences should be crystal clear and as easy to read as possible. It is a good working guideline to avoid sentences of more than 50 words. Like all such guidelines, this will occasionally be violated.

Hyperdocuments need a crisper, more modular style than traditional literature, with an emphasis on maximum clarity rather than on literary sophistication. (It might be a good idea for people creating hyperdocuments to also attempt a great novel and keep the hyperdocument simple and clear.)

SHORT PARAGRAPHS

In hypertext, long paragraphs are best avoided. As a general (violable) guideline, paragraphs should not be more than 20 lines. The author should acquire a mental habit of examining every paragraph as soon as it is written and deciding whether it could be neatly divided into separate topics. Treating each topic in a paragraph by itself helps the reader. He subconsciously digests what is in one paragraph before moving on to the next. The first sentence of each paragraph usually suggests the paragraph topic or helps the transition.

Good prose tends to mix paragraphs of different lengths. If all paragraphs are long, the prose appears heavy. If all paragraphs are short, the topics are not well cemented together. Good writing has variety; there should be both long and short paragraphs.

It is perfectly OK to use a one-sentence paragraph occasionally.

For visual appearance, there should be a blank line between each paragraph on the screen. In addition, each paragraph should begin with a word indented (either to the right or left) because, when shuffling text on a computer, two paragraphs sometimes become butted together; if there is no indentation, the paragraph break might be lost.

It would be useful if hyperdocument authoring software cautioned the author if his text in contiguous envelopes exceeded 200 lines, text in one envelope exceeded 50 lines, a paragraph exceeded 20 lines, or a sentence exceeded 50 words. The software should recommend that the author examine lengthy components to see whether they could be split.

The author should constantly scan his text to determine what could be presented better visually, for example, with bullet lists or charts. As commented upon earlier, he should constantly *categorize* and *make the categorization visual*.

ESSENTIAL BOOKS FOR WRITERS

Perhaps the best book ever written about style in writing is Strunk and White's small paperback, *The Elements of Style* [1]. The guidance offered in that book is more relevant to hyperdocuments than that found in most other books about writing English because it emphasizes a crisp, forceful style with brevity. Every author should have it. Take it around in your pocket; read it on buses and planes. Read it repeatedly until its messages are ingrained in the way you write.

A good British book on the same subject is Gower's *Plain Words* [2]. Particularly useful in this is a checklist of cautionary comments about 200 or so words and phrases which are often used badly.

Every writer should have Roget's *Thesaurus* [3] for helping find the right word or phrase and Fowler's *Modern English Usage* [4], which gives guidance about correct usage of words, phrases, and punctuation.

Because good hyperdocument nuggets have something in common with the conciseness of advertising, authors might entertain themselves by reading

- *The Art of Writing Advertisements* by Dennis Higgins [5]
- *The 100 Greatest Advertisements* by Julian Watkins [6]

Recognize, however, that advertising sometimes violates the rules of good English in order to sell. An author should not emulate its deliberate infractions of grammar, short exclamatory sentences, or attention-getting devices.

SELECTION OF TYPEFACES

Because a computer user may look at a hyperdocument screen only briefly, you should use typography that communicates as easily as possible. Selection of appropriate typefaces makes reading easier; inappropriate typefaces make it more difficult.

The human brain is a creature of habit which responds rapidly to familiar patterns. Behavioral psychologists have established that typefaces other than the most familiar retard reading. Some software allows you to select unusual typefaces with names like Old English and Specie. The more outlandish the typeface, the more difficult it is to read. Sanserif type is sometimes thought to be modern and fashionable. Serifs are the little tails which are found at the top and bottom of letters:

This is a line of type with serifs.

This is a line of type without serifs.

Normal type has serifs and lines of varying thickness. Sanserif type has no serifs and lines of constant thickness. The font name of some software lists sanserif type as "normal." The eye is trained to recognize type with serifs. John Updike comments "Serifs exist for a purpose. They help the eye pick up the shape of the letter. Piquant in little amounts, sanserif in page-size sheets repels readship like wax paper repels water." Don't use it on computer screens except for special labels.

Text which is all capital letters retards reading. The eye is accustomed to reading words in *lower case*. It may be appropriate to use capitals for a single word, but never have a whole paragraph of capitals. Headlines and bullet items on charts should be in lower case. For emphasis in headlines, use large letters— as in newspapers—not all capitals.

Never use white type on a black background, except for single phrases; it is more difficult to read than black on white.

Right justification of text makes it look neat, but experiments show that nonright-justified text is slightly easier to read.

Headlines should not have periods. Bullet items that are complete sentences should have periods.

MINIMUM NUMBER OF WORDS

An essential rule for all writing is: *Use the minimum number of words.*

Just as a machine has no unnecessary parts, so a sentence should have no unnecessary words and a paragraph no unnecessary sentences. A writer should have the mental habit of looking back over each sentence and paragraph when he has written it to work out how he could say it in fewer words.

There are two main ways to use fewer words:

- Omit needless words.

- Tighten the phraseology.

Bad: In communicating these data to your organization after fullest consultation with all my colleagues also concerned, I would certainly be less than truthful if I were to say that this has occasioned the Ministry (this section in particular) no little difficulty but the delay is nevertheless regretted [2].

Better: Sorry for the delay. We found this a difficult case.

Bad: In normal individuals the lowest concentration in which sucrose can be detected by means of gestation differs from the lowest concentration in which sucrose (in the amount employed) has to be ingested in order to produce a demonstrable decrease in olfactory acuity and a noteworthy conversion of sensations interpreted as a desire for food into sensations interpreted as a satiety associated with the ingestion of food. *(The Lancet)*

Better: A normal person can taste sugar in water in quantities so small that they do not interfere with his sense of smell or take away his appetite.

In a world of bureaucrats notorious for long memos, Winston Churchill wrote the following memo to the First Lord of the Admiralty:

Pray state this day, on one side of a sheet of paper, how the Royal Navy is being adapted to meet the conditions of modern warfare.

AVOIDANCE OF ACRONYMS

One way of compressing text which should be avoided is the casual use of acronyms.

Some branches of technology are cursed by an excessive number of acronyms. Literature in the computer industry is sometimes rendered unintelligible by alphabet soup. An author sometimes tells himself that any idiot would know the meaning of a particular acronym, but many of his readers are caught out and do not know it.

It is better for an author to write "fourth-generation language" than "4GL" even if he thinks "Everyone knows what a 4GL is."

There are some acronyms which it is not reasonable to spell out in full because the acronym is used as a product name, like IMS or OS/2. In some cases the meaning of the letters are not known. If an acronym *is* used, the text should explain what it is when it first appears. For all occurrences of it, a hyperdocument should provide a button which displays an explanatory note. The authorizing tool may build such buttons *automatically*, using a central file of acronyms for the profession in question.

AVOIDANCE OF SUPERFLUOUS WORDS

English has many superfluous words and phrases which do not enhance meaning and sometimes make prose appear stodgy. Figure 11.1 gives a list of words to be avoided.

SEQUENCE OF WORDS

In many sentences the words could be presented in alternate sequences. An author should acquire the habit of effortlessly scanning each sentence he writes to see whether the words could be sequenced better, with a change of phrasing if needed.

USE OF ACTIVE RATHER THAN PASSIVE PHRASES

Use of the active voice, rather than the passive, tends to make writing more forceful and direct.

Poor: (actual example)
The effect of this product in terms of the adequacy of the voltage suppression level to protect connected equipment has not been evaluated by Underwriters Laboratories, Inc.

Better: Underwriters Laboratories, Inc., has not evaluated whether the voltage suppression level of this product will protect connected equipment.

Verbosity in Adjectives & Adverbs:

---

true facts
acute crisis
grave emergency
active consideration
definite decision
prerequisite/essential condition
integral part
terrible disaster
real/serious danger
unduly/relatively/comparatively
respective, respectively
definite, definitely
inevitable, inevitably
particular, particularly
literally

Verbosity in Prepositions:

I'll look into the question *as to whether (whether)* you are liable.
Rates vary *in relation to (with)* the age of the child.
Similar considerations apply *with regard to (for)* application for a certificate.

as a consequence of (because of)	in the absence of (without)
by means of (by, with, using)	in the course of (during)
by virtue of (by, under)	in the event of (if)
for the purpose of (to)	in the nature of (like)
for the reason that (because)	in the neighborhood of (about)
in accordance with (by, under)	in the vicinity of (near)
in addition to (besides)	in view of (because of)
inasmuch as (since)	on the grounds of (because of)
in association with (with)	on the part of (by, among)
in case of (if)	prior to (before)
in excess of (more than, over)	subsequent to (after)
in favor of (for)	with a view to (to)
in order to (to)	with the exception of (except)

Verbosity in Adverbial and Other Phrases:

That country is not now so short of Sterling *as was formerly the case (as it used to be)*.
In the majority of cases, Most of the houses are three-bedroom.

Figure 11.1   Superfluous Words [4].

Passive:	The true facts of the case are known only to Central Committee members.
Active:	Only the Central Committee knows the truth.

Passive:	A domestic animal should not be bathed with household cleaners.
Active:	Don't wash the dog with bleach.

USE OF POSITIVE RATHER THAN NEGATIVE PHRASES

Vigorous writing generally chooses positive wording over negative wording:

Negative:	It is not often cloudy.
Positive:	It is usually sunny.

Use of the active voice to make a sentence stronger often makes it shorter, as well. The same is usually true of positive rather than negative phrasing. *Brevity is a byproduct of vigor*.

Non-Concise:	Jackson, who played the part of Geraldo, did not have the personality to make the role plausible.
Concise:	Jackson was miscast as Geraldo.

Sentences can be made exceptionally strong when positive and negative phrases about the same subject are butted together:

> Ask not what your country can do for *you*;
> ask what *you* can do for your country.
> John F. Kennedy, Inaugural Address

AVOIDANCE OF DOUBLE NEGATIVES

Negative phrasing often makes sentences weaker than they should be; double negatives make them still weaker and should almost never be used.

Poor:	Do not delay returning this form because you do not know your National Insurance number. [2]
Better:	Send back this form at once, even if you do not know your National Insurance number.

In some cases, they make sentences confusing:

> *Poor:*   Inability to discuss the theory behind the product is not impeding more than 45 percent of our salesmen.
>
> *Better:*   Fifty-five percent of our salesmen are impeded by inability to discuss the theory of the product.

USE OF BOLDFACE AND ITALIC CHARACTERS

When a new technical word is introduced, put it in **boldface** or *italic* to draw the reader's attention to it:

> The computer may also use a key which does not uniquely identify a record, but which identifies all those records which have a certain property. This is referred to as a **secondary key** or **search key**. A value of the attribute "color" may be used as a secondary key (e.g., "blue").

Italics should be used for highlighting differences:

> The greater the rate of introduction of new technology the greater the need to protect the old existing applications from it. This is one of the main reasons why we need *database* systems rather than *file* systems with no data independence.

Italics should be used for *special emphasis:*

> It is often easy for a systems analyst to imagine that the data structure he has designed for an application is stable and, because he has left spare bytes, will not need to be changed. *Time and time again, he is proven wrong.* The requirements change in unforeseen ways. The larger the base of application programs, the more expensive these changes can be.

DOUBLE MEANINGS

English sentences can easily have more than one meaning. A writer should examine his sentences instinctively checking whether a reader could misinterpret them:

> I have discussed the question of stocking the proposed poultry plant with my colleagues. [2]
>
> Prices of different models vary, and you should take the advice of an expert on the make. [2]

Sometimes double meanings, or incorrect meaning, are caused by inappropriate positioning of words in the sentence:

> If the cat does not like raw fish, fry it.
>
> She took a piece of silk from the table, unfolded it, and displayed an altar cloth of her own exquisite embroidery, upon which everyone began to blow their nose. [5]

PUNCTUATION CAUSING INCORRECT MEANING

The incorrect positioning of commas can give a sentence incorrect meaning:

> Teenagers, who drive dangerously, should not be allowed to have a license.

The foregoing sentence implies that all teenagers drive dangerously. The commas should be deleted.

USE OF DEFINITE, SPECIFIC, CONCRETE LANGUAGE

Strunk and White advise, "Prefer the specific to the general, the definite to the vague, the concrete to the abstract." They quote a passage from the Bible translated by George Orwell into the type of bloodless prose one finds in contemporary papers:

Orwell's Version:	"Objective consideration of contemporary phenomena compels the conclusion that success or failure in competitive activities exhibits no tendency to be commensurate with innate capacity, but that a considerable element of the unpredictable must inevitably be taken into account."
King James Version:	"I saw that the race is not to the swift, nor the battle to the strong, neither yet bread to the wise, not yet riches to men of understanding, nor yet favor to men of skill; but time and chance happeneth to them all."

The writer should be specific and describe illustrations which make the reader pay attention. He should look for concrete examples to illustrate generalities. These help the reader to understand. Great writers choose words which are concrete, definite, and specific.

FINDING ILLUSTRATIONS THAT STAY IN THE READERS' MINDS

A writer should search for examples, illustrations, analogies, and comparisons that are dramatic so that the reader will remember them. Much of the writing in textbooks and papers is boring because it is colorless. The writer does not use concrete examples or find illustrations which stop the reader in his or her tracks. The readers's mind glides over the prose without registering much. Good writers grasp the attention of the reader with illustrations which stay in the reader's head. Their words conjure up pictures.

> "During the past hour, 12,000 children have been born around the world. 60% have come into households where income per head is lower than $350 a year which the European Economic Community pays in annual subsidy for each cow."
> *The Economist,* December 24, 1988

> "You have witchcraft in your lips, Kate; there is more eloquence in a sugar touch of them than in the tongues of the French council."
> Shakespeare, *King Henry V*

> "Special-purpose devices have been built that exploit parallelism to perform specific tasks quickly. Like idiot savants, however, such machines are usually quite awkward outside their specialties. In contrast, the Connection Machine can operate at its peak processing rate in a wide range of applications."
> Daniel Hillis, *The Connection Machine* [7]

AVOIDANCE OF SENTENCES WITH MANY CONNECTIVES

Long lists of items separated by commas or semicolons should be broken into bullet lists.

> *Poor:* An envelope can contain text, diagrams, images like photographs, animated diagrams, spreadsheets with spreadsheet software, sound, television or videos displayed in a window, expert systems, programs, or combinations of them.
>
> *Better:* An envelope can contain
>
> - text
> - diagrams
> - images like photographs
> - animated diagrams

- spreadsheets with spreadsheet software
- sound
- television (or video displayed in a window)
- expert systems
- programs
- combinations of the foregoing

When the list is more than seven items, the author should see whether it can be split into subcategories. For example, in the foregoing case,

Possible contents of an envelope:
- displayed information
  - text
  - diagrams
  - images like photographs
  - animated diagrams
  - sound
  - television (or video displayed in a window)
- programs
  - spreadsheets with spreadsheet software
  - expert systems
  - other programs
  - combinations of the foregoing

Breaking strings of items with connectives into bullet lists is one way of creating visual patterns which help the reader to organize ideas.

VISUAL LAYOUT

Because hyperdocuments are, in part, a *visual* medium, words may be arranged in patterns on the screen when this is useful:

Original:	Programmed routines built into hyperdocuments can be activated when the document is first opened, when an envelope of the document is opened, or when a button is activated.
Improvement:	Programmed routines built into hyperdocuments can be activated:

- when the document is opened
- when an envelope is opened
- when a button is activated

To help the reader organize ideas, similar phrases may be arranged vertically so that similar words line up. The following advice about choice of words follows this guideline:

Prefer the familiar word to the unfamiliar.

Prefer the concrete word to the abstract.

Prefer the short word to the long.

Prefer the single word to the phrase.

The creation of visual patterns is more important in hyperdocuments than in text. It is often useful to use the computer screen like the screen of a seminar presenter.

METAPHORS

Well-chosen metaphors can have a conciseness and power that other words cannot. Winston Churchill used them masterfully:

> Dictators ride to and fro upon tigers which they dare not dismount. And the tigers are getting hungry.
>
> An iron curtain has descended across the Continent.
>
> . . . the soft underbelly of the Axis.

Mixed metaphors, on the other hand, can appear ludicrous:

> Shooting down sacred cows.
> The sacred cows have come home to roost.
> The road to Braintree has not yet got off the ground.
> Anyone making concrete forecasts is liable to come unstuck.
> Neurocomputing is a virgin field pregnant with opportunities.

A metaphor may accidentally clash with nonmetaphor words. Sentences like the following should be avoided:

> The working man is being squeezed flat by inflation.
>
> Persons with diarrhea and vomiting should not be allowed to swamp the emergency medical services.

Overworked metaphors can make writing seem pompous:

> . . . exploring every avenue.
> . . . leaving no stone unturned.
> . . . when the chips are down.

Metaphors should be used sparingly, but an author should always be asking himself whether a well-used metaphor can make his text clearer and more fun. Metaphors can be a surprise to the reader which makes the text more enjoyable to read.

> *Poor:*   Some documents were authored with paucity of coherent thought resulting in an absence of structured paradigms the lack of which causes the conversion effort to be fraught with frustrations.
>
> *Better (if the style is used sparingly):*
>
> Some documents are sows' ears, and it will be a frustrating task to turn them into silk purses.

CRITIQUE AND POLISH

Every author needs to read his sentences, paragraphs, and chapters critically as soon as he has written them.

- Search for possible misinterpretations.
- Search for ways to lessen the number of words.
- Search for better structures.
- Search for the possibility of using charts and diagrams.
- Search for greater clarity.
- Search for more powerful words or metaphors.
- Above all, put yourself in the head of the reader. Try to understand his or her feelings, criticisms, and needs. Adjust the prose and diagrams with the reader in mind.

The author should have four types of people critique his work:

- A copy editor or people good with words.
- A picture editor or people good with diagrams.
- Experts on the subject matter.
- People who are the target audience.

The author should solicit comments on hyperdocuments from people who use the hyperdocument itself and are experienced with what constitutes good hyperdocuments, as well as from people who critique a paper version of the material.

T. S. Eliot wrote about the importance of criticism in the work of creation:

"Probably the larger part of the labor of an author in composing his work is critical labor; the labor of sifting, combining, constructing, expunging, correcting, testing: this frightful toil is as much critical as creative." [8]

12 CLARITY IN THE USE OF DIAGRAMS

INTRODUCTION   Diagrams, as we have stressed, are a vital part of hyperdocuments. When used well, they communicate information more powerfully than most text. Items on diagrams should be designed to hyperlink to other diagrams and text.

It is important to think of hyperdocuments as a *visual* medium. They organize nuggets of information into structures for fast navigation. Many of these nuggets should include graphics.

Most manuals and textbooks are full of ideas which can be portrayed as charts. Often, what is text would communicate better if it were charts. The hyperdocument author should read his text critically and ask himself, "Could I put that into charts?"

Just as hyperdocuments demand concise and clear English, so also do they need concise and clear diagrams. This chapter (and the next two) are concerned with how to create good diagrams.

TRYING OUT   Devising the clearest diagrams is an art which a cre-
DIFFERENT   ator of hyperdocuments needs to learn. Once a per-
STRUCTURES   son has learned the principles of good communica-
                     tion in diagrams, he will learn to spot faults in many
of the diagrams he sees in academic papers, books, and magazines. Many of these do not communicate as well as they should.

For any one diagram there may be many possible structures, formats, and layouts. The author should experiment with these, possibly drawing the diagram many ways, selecting which is best, and polishing its details. Diagrams are almost always going to improve if they go through editing, revision, and testing against different design options.

As stressed in Chapter 6, the author may be assisted by an artist or graphics editor who has a sense of graphics design, knows how to communicate powerfully with diagrams, and is fast and skilled with one or more computerized graphics tools. A managing editor inspecting an author's hyperdocument should examine the diagrams first. This can be done quickly, and improvements can usually be suggested.

The first rule in creating diagrams, then, is to *experiment,* revise, polish, test with other people. Much improvement in clarity will result.

T. S. Eliot's statement about authoring prose is even more relevant to authoring diagrams: "Probably the larger part of the labor of an author in composing his work is critical labor; the labor of sifting, combining, constructing, expunging, correcting, testing"[1].

SELF-EXPLANATORY PORTRAYAL OF COMPLEXITY

Complex subjects can be made easy to understand by the use of multiple, well-designed diagrams. The task of the author in creating diagrams is to give visual clarity to something subtle, complex, or difficult to explain in print. The objective of diagrams is to achieve the clearest possible portrayal of complexity.

The worst act of a graphic designer is to make something which is basically simple appear complicated.

The caption and the labels need to be crystal clear. Take the time to examine alternate forms of wording, and select the best. Captions and labels must be concise. Use the minimum number of words (but no fewer).

We emphasized that the viewer may reach a diagram by many paths; he may or may not have read the text which accompanies the diagram. Therefore, the diagram must be understandable in its own right and must be accompanied by a self-explanatory caption.

USE OF NO MORE THAN SEVEN ITEMS ON A CHART WHERE POSSIBLE

Chapter 9 alluded to the fact that human short-term memory, which we use when communicating or thinking about problems, has a capacity to retain about seven different items. Where possible, a chart should contain no more than seven pieces of information. Seven items are enough for a bullet list, seven blocks are enough on a chart, and so on. More complex charts should be subdivided, if possible, either sequentially or hierarchically. Long lists should be made into hierarchies as shown in Figs. 9.1 and 9.2.

USE OF NO MORE THAN SEVEN CATEGORIES ON A SCALE

As well as being able to remember seven "chunks" of information, we are able to identify about seven divisions on a scale.

Psychologists have conducted experiments using undimensional data[1]. The subject is briefly shown a point on a linear scale between two markers and is asked to judge its *position*. Tones of different *frequencies* are played for the subject, and he is asked to assign numerals to them. The subject is played tones of different *volumes*, is shown different *colors*, or is asked to identify items on other undimensional scales. If he has to choose from a range of three or four alternatives, he answers correctly every time. If, however, he has to choose from a range of twenty alternatives, he answers incorrectly every time, because the range exceeds the bandwidth of his channel for perception. In many cases, seven alternatives are the approximate limit of his channel capacity.

Long before any such experiments, man had used seven divisions for a variety of undimensional scales. We define seven primary colors in a continuous spectrum of light. Psychologists and sociologists have long used seven-point rating scales. There are seven days in the week, seven ages of man, and seven levels of hell!

We should not expect our hyperdocument viewer to differentiate between more than seven categories on an undimensional scale. Some charts have required a viewer to distinguish between ten levels of gray or more than seven colors. These do not communicate effectively.

USE OF COLORS

Diagrams can be improved greatly by using two colors (say, black and red). You can say things on a color diagram which would be best avoided on a monochrome diagram.

Color can be used for emphasis and to separate different types of information. It can help to make a diagram visually simpler by making the reader digest the black part before studying the colored part. It can put rich collections of information on data maps.

I had a major battle with my textbook publishers to persuade them to publish the books in two colors. The use of two colors gave me more scope in creating clear diagrams.

While two colors can aid clarity, many colors can cause confusion. It is usually difficult to extract information from a diagram as colorful as a Christmas tree. The mind does not readily give a visual ordering to multiple colors. Shades of gray indicate levels of intensity or importance; multiple colors do not.

Some viewers are color-blind; however, they distinguish clearly between red and black. They usually distinguish blue from other colors. Red, blue, black, and white might be acceptable for mnemonic encoding but not more colors than these.

Although computer graphics tools make it easy to generate charts rich with color, the need to communicate well should override the urge to decorate colorfully.

BUILDING UP TO   Sometimes it is necessary to have complex diagrams
COMPLEX CHARTS   with far more than seven items. Complex diagrams
                     designed with skill can often express information
with much greater power than text. At the first sight of a complex and unfamiliar diagram, the viewer might react by thinking that it is too difficult to bother with. He may skip it to look at more appealing items. Because of this, it is a good idea to introduce the complexity a step at a time. Complex diagrams may be built up in stages.

Figure 12.1 is a graphic which conveys a large amount of information concisely. It is a schedule of trains between Paris and Lyon in the 1880s[2]. It would be useful if books of airline schedules could have similar charts. Some viewers, however, look at Fig. 12.1 with the initial reaction that it is too complicated. In a hyperdocument, the viewer might be shown a chart with one train first so that he learns the grammar of the chart.

Figure 12.2 shows an introductory diagram which a viewer might see before looking at Fig. 12.1.

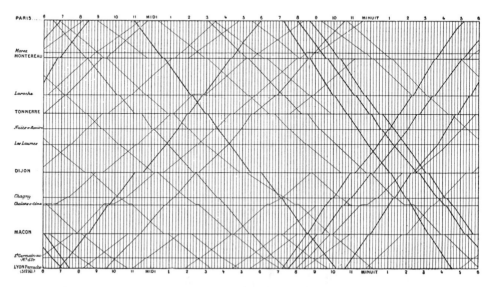

Figure 12.1 Train schedule from Paris to Lyon in the 1880s. (From E. J. Marey, *La Méthode Graphique,* Paris, 1885, p. 20, in Tufte. p. 31. The method is attributed to the French engineer, Ibry.)

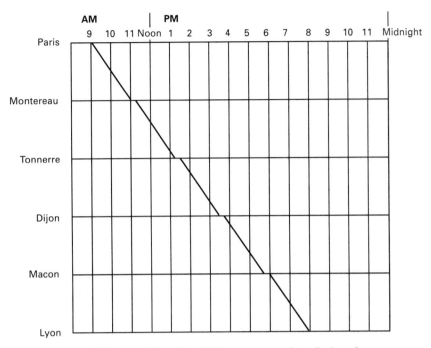

Figure 12.2   Schedule of the 9:20 A.M. express from Paris to Lyon.

BREAKDOWN OF COMPLEX CHARTS

Conversely, the viewer might be given the ability to decompose a complex diagram, at the touch of a button, into simpler diagrams which are easier to grapple with.

Figure 12.3, for example, is a diagram summarizing the arguments in a hyperdocument about trade-offs in telecommunications satellite design. The entire document is built around the structure in Fig. 12.3. When the viewer asks to see the buttons in Fig. 12.3, the computer rapidly displays a button around each block, one at a time. Activating any one of them results in a simpler display showing the block in question and what is connected to it. Figure 12.4 shows the effect of "pressing" the button around "Satellite Antenna Size."

Once a designer has built Fig. 12.3 with a computerized drawing tool, he can quickly create a family of diagrams like Fig. 12.4 by deleting parts of the original. Figure 12.4 might have five buttons, one for each the links, which put labels on the chart explaining the nature of the trade-offs.

HAVING A STORY TO TELL

Good diagrams tell a story. Their designer needs to understand what the story is and to tell it as clearly as possible. Often the story is best told with a sequence

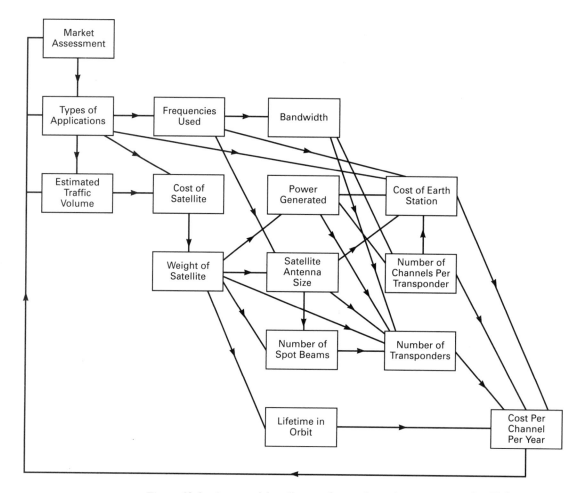

Figure 12.3 An organizing diagram from a hyperdocument on trade-offs in telecommunications satellite design. A button is displayable around each of the blocks. "Pressing" the button on Satellite Antenna Size causes a simpler diagram to be displayed, showing the links to that block. (See Fig. 12.4.)

of diagrams hyperlinked together. Pop-on explanations are an important part of the storytelling.

The author designs text with hierarchical structures and envelope diagrams. He should design the graphics and the story they tell in a similar fashion.

Figure 12.5 shows a structure for the segment about satellite trade-offs. The hierarchical breakdown in Fig. 12.5 is useful, but it does not reveal the interwoven relationships that are in Fig. 12.3. Figure 12.3 is an organizing structure around which most of the document is built. Figure 12.3 hyperlinks into multiple segments which are part of the storytelling.

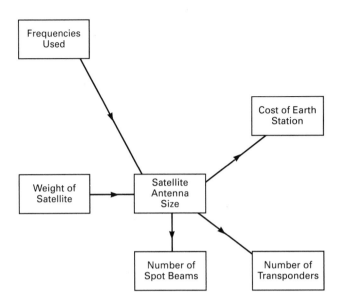

Figure 12.4 Trade-offs in satellite design relating to satellite antenna size. A subset of Figure 12.3 is displayed when a viewer activates the button around Satellite Antenna Size.

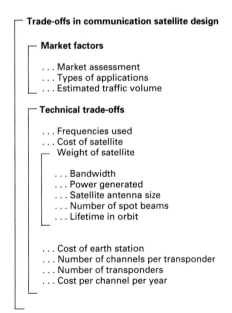

Figure 12.5 Hierarchical breakdown for segment about satellite trade-offs.

HIERARCHIES

Certain types of information are best represented in hierarchies. A hierarchy can be drawn in six different ways:

- Top-down tree
- Left-to-right tree
- Table with columns
- Set of nested boxes
- Bracket diagram
- Indented list

A Top-Down Tree

Figure 12.6 shows a top-down tree. This is the most common way of drawing a hierarchy. It has the disadvantage that, if it is a large hierarchy, it tends to spread horizontally.

A Left-To-Right Tree

A tree structure can be turned on its side as shown in Fig. 12.7. It tends to spread vertically rather than horizontally. It can be examined with vertical scrolling on the computer screen.

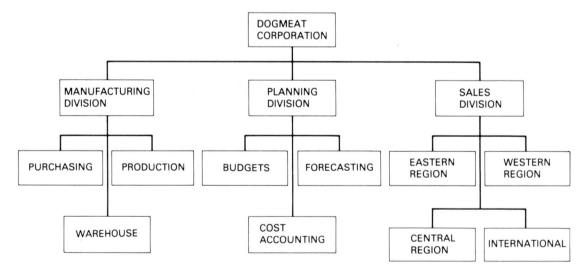

Figure 12.6 A top-down tree is the most common way of drawing a hierarchical structure.

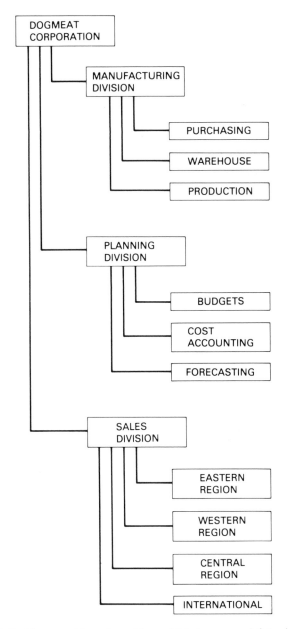

Figure 12.7 The same hierarchy as Figure 12.6 drawn as a left-to-right tree.

A Table with Columns

Figure 12.8 shows the same tree drawn as a table of columns.

A Set of Nested Boxes

Figure 12.9 shows the tree drawn as a set of nested boxes. This is rarely done.

Bracket Diagram

Figure 12.10 shows a bracket diagram with which we are now familiar. This is really the left-hand side of a diagram like Fig. 12.9. It can be manipulated rapidly with bracket-diagram editors.

An Indented List

Figure 12.11 shows Fig. 12.10 with the brackets removed, representing the hierarchy as an indented list.

WEB STRUCTURES Charts connecting blocks into a web are more complex than a hierarchy. They are often drawn in an ill-structured fashion (as shown in Fig. 12.12). In such charts, there are usually blocks with common properties which ought (for clarity) to be grouped together. Any web structure can be divided into hierarchical structures with cross-links.

DOGMEAT CORPORATION										
MANUFACTURING DIVISION			PLANNING DIVISION			SALES DIVISION				
PURCHASING	PRODUCTION	WAREHOUSE	BUDGETS	FORECASTING	COST ACCOUNTING	EASTERN REGION	WESTERN REGION	CENTRAL REGION	INTERNATIONAL	

Figure 12.8 Tree drawn as a table of columns.

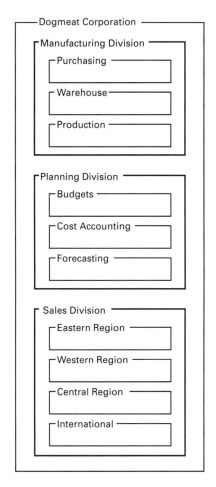

Figure 12.9 Tree drawn as a set of nested boxes.

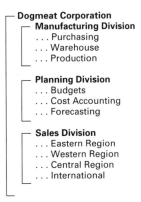

Figure 12.10 Bracket diagram.

Dogmeat Corporation
  Manufacturing Division
    Purchasing
    Warehouse
    Production

  Planning Division
    Budgets
    Cost Accounting
    Forecasting

  Sales Division
    Eastern Region
    Western Region
    Central Region
    International   *Figure 12.11*   An indented list.

Representing it as hierarchies often makes it clearer. Any nonhierarchical web can be divided into hierarchies in more than one way. The author should experiment with these different forms and decide which represents the information most clearly.

Figure 12.13, for example, redraws Fig. 12.12 in two different ways.

Sometimes complex web structures should be broken up hierarchically by means of nesting. Figure 12.14, for example, shows a web structure with more than seven blocks. It can be nested into two separate diagrams as shown in Fig. 12.15. Here the right-hand diagram is an expansion of the lowest block on the left-hand diagram. To indicate the nesting, the blocks in the right-hand diagram have been renumbered.

Figure 12.15 is less spaghettilike than Fig. 12.14. This becomes important when webs with large numbers of blocks are drawn, especially if they are to be

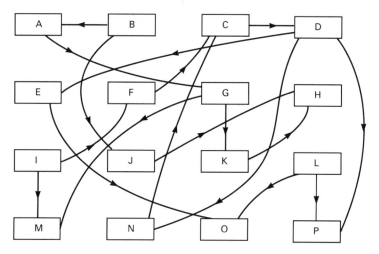

Figure 12.12   A web (mesh-structured or network-structured) diagram. This would become a mess if it had a large number of nodes. (Imagine 600 nodes.)

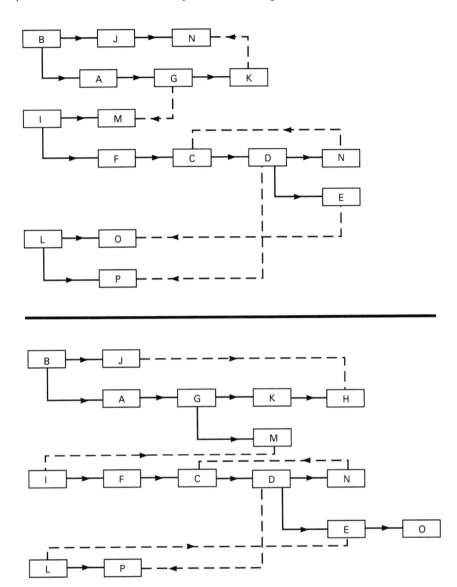

Figure 12.13   Figure 12.12 redrawn in two ways. The dotted lines are links connecting hierarchies. Any web structure can be broken into hierarchies with cross-links.

viewed on a relatively small computer screen. In general, an author should experiment with complex structures to find the ones which communicate his messages in the clearest fashion.

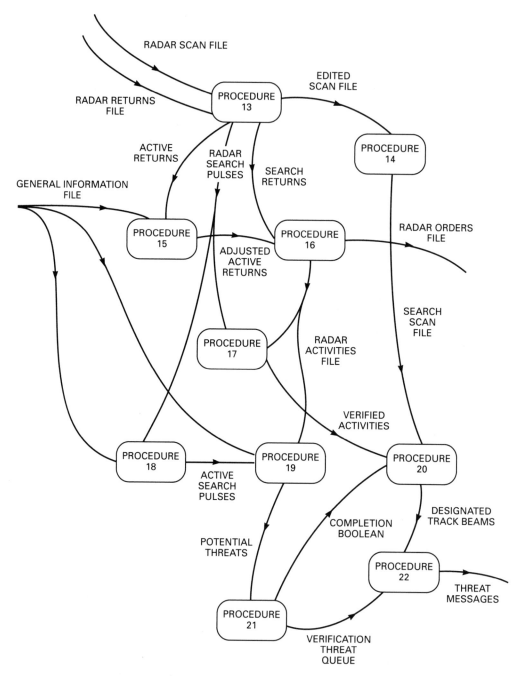

Figure 12.14 Web structure with more than seven blocks. This can be broken into two diagrams as shown in Fig 12.15.

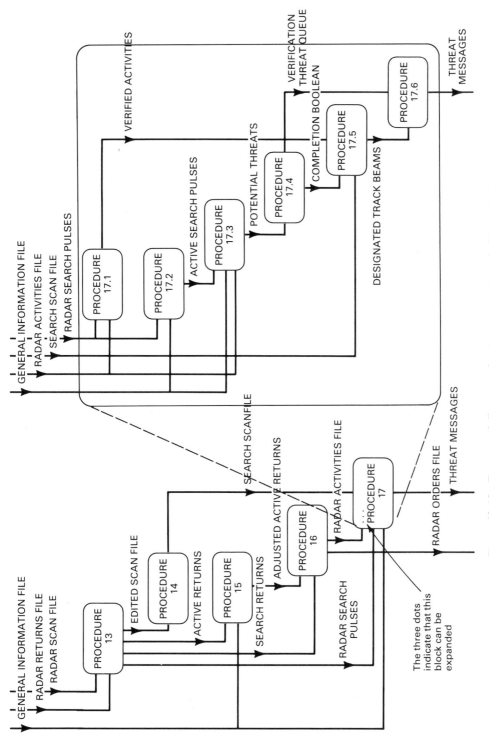

Figure 12.15 Two nested diagrams of web structure shown in Figure 12.14. Procedures 17 to 22 in Fig 12.14 have become Procedures 17.1 to 17.6 here.

141

AVOIDANCE OF DECORATION Diagrams in hypermedia should be as concise and crisp as possible. Just as it is good practice in writing (especially in writing hyperdocuments) to minimize the number of words used, so is it good practice in diagramming to convey the ideas as concisely as possible.

Some authors create diagrams with various forms of decoration. It is easy to generate decorative effects with computerized tools such as Ashton-Tate's Applause. Decoration often detracts from the precise message of the diagram and should be avoided.

MAXIMIZING THE DATA/PIXEL RATIO Edward Tufte, who has written one of the best books ever on graphical design, distinguishes between *data ink* and *nondata ink* on charts[3]. Data ink is not erasable without removing data from the charts. Nondata ink can be removed, and the chart will still show the data.

One of Tufte's principles is that the *data/ink ratio* should be maximized.

$$\text{data/ink ratio} = \frac{\text{data ink}}{\text{total ink used to print the graphic}}$$

Most graphics contain ink which can be removed without losing information, and when it is removed, the graphic is often clearer. Tufte states: "Every bit of ink on a graphic requires a reason. And nearly always that reason should be that the ink presents new information." With screen diagrams, the equivalent phrase would be *data/pixel ratio*.

If A = total number of pixels that could *not* be removed without removing data and N = total number of pixels activated in a display, the

$$\text{data/pixel ratio} = \frac{A}{N}$$

Computerized "draw" and "paint" tools make it easy to fill a display with visual clutter which detracts from, rather than enhances, the main message of the diagram. The data/pixel ratio should be kept low.

EXAMPLE OF MAXIMIZING THE DATA/PIXEL RATIO Tufte uses the following illustration from Linus Pauling's book *General Chemistry*[4]:*

---

*From *General Chemistry 3/e* by Linus Pauling. Copyright © 1947, 1950, 1953, 1970 by Linus Pauling. Reprinted by permission of W.H. Freeman and Company.

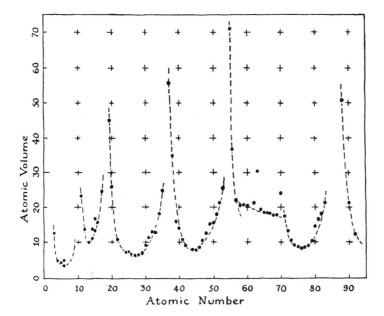

The grid crosses and part of the frame can be removed—this part:

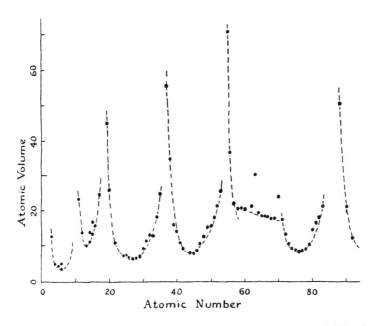

When they are removed, something important becomes visible that might have been unobserved in the original: several of the elements do not fit the smooth theoretical curves.

On a hyperdiagram, a button should be displayable which, when activated, points out and explains this phenomenon.

When a chart is cleaned up in this way, there is room to include other data which might be valuable. For example, the rare earths which do not fit a smooth curve should be labeled. The initial elements in each period might be labeled:

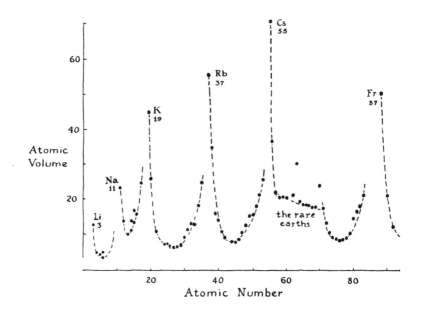

Here the label of the vertical axis has been made horizontal, making it slightly more "friendly."

ARTISTIC DIARRHEA

In many cases, the basic message of a chart is drowned in unnecessary artwork. This is often true in news magazines.

The following chart tends to hide what little information it contains[5]:

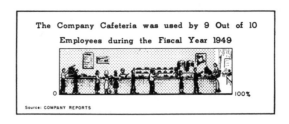

Chart specialists for some magazines have an art school background rather than training in statistics. Their artwork often hides rather than clarifies the facts. Edward Tufte refers to unnecessary decoration as "chartjunk." Chartjunk is not a new phenomenon. Jonathan Swift condemned the illustrations with elephants and other imagery that seventeenth-century cartographers would put on their maps:

> With savage pictures fill their gaps
> And o'er unhabitable downs
> Place elephants for want of towns.

Louis Silverstein of the *New York Times* commented "at least *we* don't put naked women in our graphics"[6].

Computerized charting tools encourage a new form of artistic diarrhea. They provide the capability to instantly fill diagrams with fancy colors and shading like fishscales or carpet designs (Fig. 12.16). Casual use of such facilities, like casual decoration, lessens the communication power of the diagram.

Some computer software produces what its advertisers refer to as three-dimensional charts. It is possible with this to create vividly colorful charts which convey information poorly. Figure 12.17 is an example taken from a vendor's advertising.

Figure 12.16 Computerized tools for creating graphics make it easy to fill the screen with patterns that distract from, rather than enhance, the message of the chart. They need to be used with a sense of communication skill.

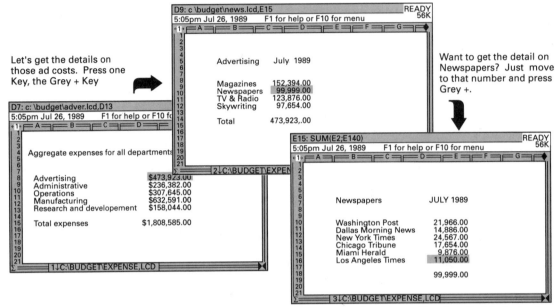

Let's get the details on those ad costs. Press one Key, the Grey + Key

Want to get the detail on Newspapers? Just move to that number and press Grey +.

D9: c \budget\news.lcd,E15 — READY 56K
5:05pm Jul 26, 1989   F1 for help or F10 for menu

	A	B	C	D	E	G

Advertising   July 1989

Magazines   152,394.00
Newspapers   99,999.00
TV & Radio   123,876.00
Skywriting   97,654.00

Total   473,923,.00

2↓C:\BUDGET\EXPEN

D7: c: \budget\adver.lcd,D13
5:05pm Jul 26, 1989   F1 for help or F10 f

Aggregate expenses for all departments

Advertising $473,923.00
Administrative $236,382.00
Operations $307,645.00
Manufacturing $632,591.00
Research and developement $158,044.00

Total expenses $1,808,585.00

1↓C:\BUDGET\EXPENSE,LCD

E15: SUM(E2;E140) — READY 56K
5:05pm Jul 26, 1989   F1 for help or F10 for menu

	A	B	C	D	E	F	G

Newspapers   JULY 1989

Washington Post   21,966.00
Dallas Morning News   14,886.00
New York Times   24,567.00
Chicago Tribune   17,654.00
Miami Herald   9,876.00
Los Angeles Times   11,050.00

99,999.00

3↓C:\BUDGET\EXPENSE,LCD

Here we are on level three. There's no limit to the levels you can move down.

Bingo does multiple windows. Notice: different drives, directories, down many 3-D levels. All at the same time!

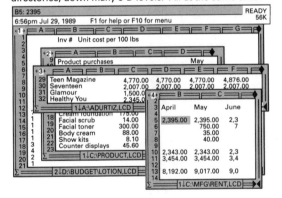

B5: 2395 — READY 56K
6:56pm Jul 29, 1989   F1 for help or F10 for menu

Inv # Unit cost per 100 lbs

Product purchases   May

	Teen Magazine	Seventeen	Glamour	Healthy You
29	4,770.00	4,770.00	4,770.00	4,876.00
30	2,007.00	2,007.00	2,007.00	2,007.00
31	1,500.00			
32	2,345.0			

1↓A:\ADURTIZ,LCD

Cream foundation   175.00
Facial scrub   14.00
Facial toner   300.00
Body cream   88.00
Show kits   8.10
Counter displays   45.60

April   May   June
2,395.00   2,395.00   2,3
750.00   7
35.00
40.00
2,343.00   2,343.00   2,3
3,454.00   3,454.00   3,4
8,192.00   9,017.00   9,0

1↓C:\PRODUCT,LCD
2↓D:\BUDGET\LOTION,LCD
1↓C:\MFG\RENT,LCD

Here, we popped Bingo up over Word Perfect. Then we pumped those figures into a letter on-the-fly with the Clipboard. Click,click—that quick!

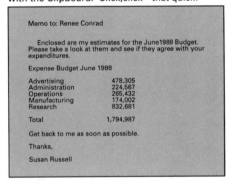

Memo to: Renee Conrad

Enclosed are my estimates for the June1988 Budget. Please take a look at them and see if they agree with your expenditures.

Expense Budget June 1988

Advertising   478,305
Administration   224,567
Operations   265,432
Manufacturing   174,002
Research   832,681

Total   1,794,987

Get back to me as soon as possible.

Thanks,

Susan Russell

Figure 12.17   Computer-generated three-dimensional chart.

**WHERE
REDUNDANT
PIXELS ARE
USEFUL**

It is a valuable mental discipline to maximize the data/pixel ratio; however in certain cases redundant pixels can add to the ability of the diagram to communicate information.

Redundant pixels can be used to emphasize important parts of a diagram. An important box, for example, may be drawn with bold lines, red shading, or a black shadow:

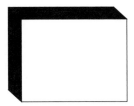

Some lines may be thicker than other lines to show emphasis.

Sometimes shading, shadows, or color add to the visual impact of a diagram. They may increase the desire of the viewer to want to study the diagram, or may increase the likelihood of her remembering the diagram.

In Fig. 12.18, the intense black shading increases the power of the chart. It suggests the idea of signal loss. It may make the viewer remember the chart.

**RECOMMENDED
TECHNIQUE**

A useful approach to improving the value of diagrams, then, is to:

- Remove nondata pixels, where appropriate.
- Remove redundant pixels.
- Maximize the data/pixel ratio.
- Add nondata or redundant pixels to give valuable emphasis to important items.
- Add nondata or redundant pixels to increase the visual impact or ability of the diagram to communicate.

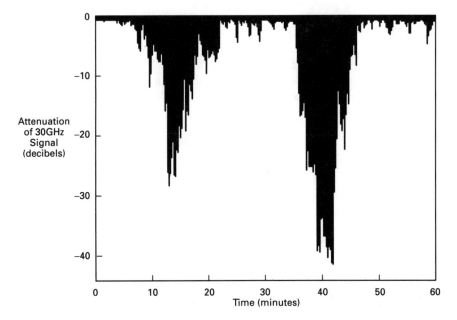

Figure 12.18   Attenuation of 30-GHz transmission caused by abnormally in-tense rainstorms (exceeding 100 millimeters per hour). Attenuation of more than 30 decibels is not more than a few minutes in duration. The black shad-ing conveys the idea of signal loss and gives the chart more visual impact.

13 GRAPHICAL DISPLAY OF NUMERIC DATA

TOOLS FOR NUMERICAL CHARTING

A particularly important type of diagram is that which displays numeric data. Many computerized tools exist for creating numeric charts. Some of them are parts of spreadsheet tools. Some are tools for creating presentations. Hyperdocuments software should make it easy to hyperlink to and from the charts made with such tools.

Figure 13.1 shows typical examples of the types of charts common in software for displaying numerical data.

The principles of Chapter 10 apply to numeric charts as well as to other diagrams. The charts should be clearly captioned and self-explanatory. They should use buttons to display explanations of anything that might require explaining. The author should resist decoration and patterns which detract from the basic meaning of the chart.

GRAPHICS REVEAL DATA

Humans are generally better at pattern recognition than computers. Computers can quickly produce means, standard deviations, correlation coefficients, and so on, but a chart can reveal that information visually.

Consider the sets of numbers shown as Table 13.1. When the numbers are plotted, they appear as in Fig. 13.2[1]. The reader looking at these charts immediately knows much more about the sets of numbers. Looking at plots he can immediately spot exceptions, which might be errors, such as the outlying points in charts III and IV.

Simple Bar Chart

Grouped Bar Chart

Stacked Bar Chart

Horizontal Bar Chart

Figure 13.1 Typical charts common in software for displaying numerical data.

Line Chart

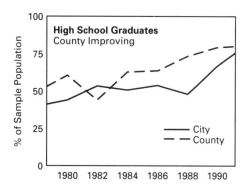

Profit/Loss Area Chart

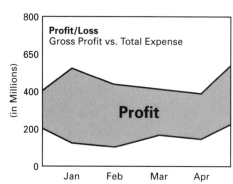

Pie Chart

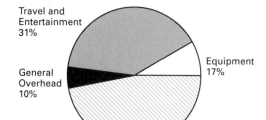

Mixed Chart

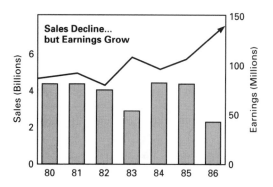

Figure 13.1   (continued)

Table 13.1

I		II		III		IV	
X	Y	X	Y	X	Y	X	Y
10.0	8.04	10.0	9.14	10.0	7.46	8.0	6.58
8.0	6.95	8.0	8.14	8.0	6.77	8.0	5.76
13.0	7.58	13.0	8.74	13.0	12.74	8.0	7.71
9.0	8.81	9.0	8.77	9.0	7.11	8.0	8.84
11.0	8.33	11.0	9.26	11.0	7.81	8.0	8.47
14.0	9.96	14.0	8.10	14.0	8.84	8.0	7.04
6.0	7.24	6.0	6.13	6.0	6.08	8.0	5.25
4.0	4.26	4.0	3.10	4.0	5.39	19.0	12.50
12.0	10.84	12.0	9.13	12.0	8.15	8.0	5.56
7.0	4.82	7.0	7.26	7.0	6.42	8.0	7.91
5.0	5.68	5.0	4.74	5.0	5.73	8.0	6.89

Statistics provide the following information about these numbers:

number of samples in each set $= 11$

mean of X's $= 9.0$

mean of Y's $= 7.5$

equation of regression line: $Y = 3 + 0.5X$

standard error of estimate of slope $= 0.118$

$t = 4.24$

sum of squares $X - \overline{X} = 110.0$

regression sum of squares $= 27.50$

residual sum of squares of $Y = 13.75$

correlation coefficient $= 0.82$

$r^2 = 0.67$

ELABORATE GRAPHICAL PLOTS   Computers can generate charts which are more elaborate than those an author could generate by hand. They can also generate charts which are confusing. The goal of the author must be to reveal information in the powerful nonconfusing way.

Figure 13.3 shows computer-generated charts which reveal information better than tables, text, and hand-drawn charts[2].

Data maps can be a particularly valuable form of computer-generated chart. Figure 13.4 shows an example[3]. Data maps can be more useful if colors are used.

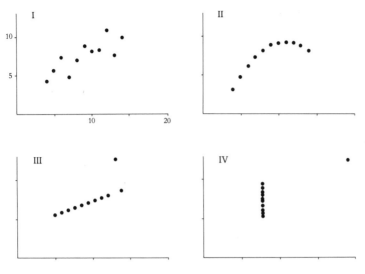

Figure 13.2

CAUSE AND EFFECT

Many charts display causes and effects. When this is done, it is a useful convention to put the cause on the horizontal axis and the effect on the vertical axis.

For the charts, a horizontal rather than a vertical frame is appropriate. Ideally, it should fit neatly into the computer screen and not need scrolling. For a few charts, a vertical frame will be more appropriate.

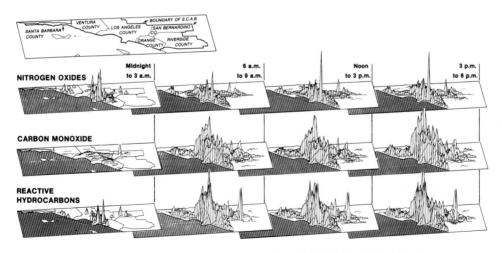

Figure 13.3 Computer-generated charts. Copyright © 1979, Los Angeles Times. Reprinted by permission.

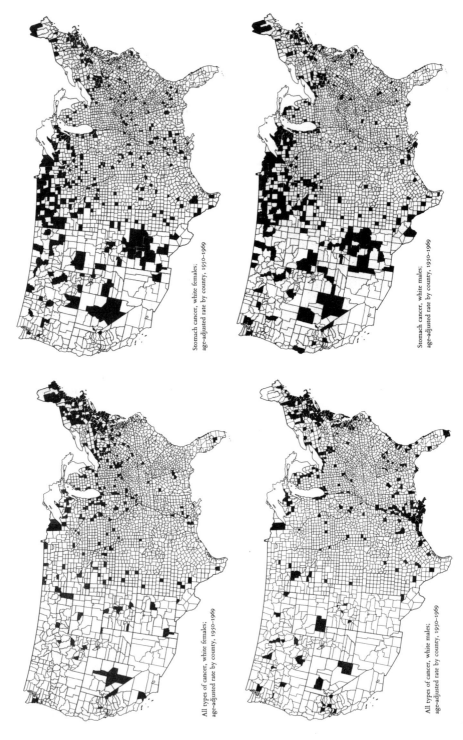

Stomach cancer, white females;
age-adjusted rate by county, 1950–1969

Stomach cancer, white males;
age-adjusted rate by county, 1950–1969

All types of cancer, white females;
age-adjusted rate by county, 1950–1969

All types of cancer, white males;
age-adjusted rate by county, 1950–1969

Figure 13.4   Data maps can be very effective in color.

Sometimes it is useful to draw numeric charts which are beyond the scope of typical charting software. The train schedule in Fig. 12.1 is an elegant chart that would have to be constructed with "draw" software rather than with charting software.

Figure 13.5 is a helpful chart. In drawing charts about the evolution of technology, it is useful to have a log scale. Most charting

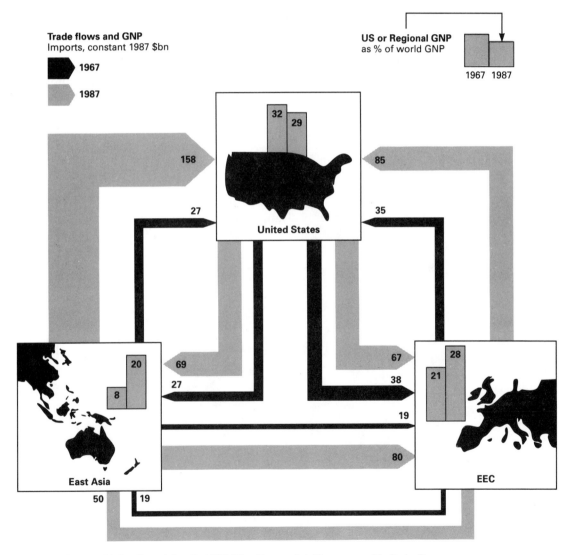

Figure 13.5 Copyright © 1988 The Economist Newspaper Limited. Reprinted with permission.

software cannot draw the shading illustrated in Figure 13.6, nor can it draw log scales.

In most cases, a picture *is* worth a thousand words. A graphic gives more insight than a table of numbers. Often, the table is needed as well as the graphic because it contains valuable detail. The viewer should be able to hyperlink from the graphic to the table of source numbers.

Sometimes a graphic is not the best form of representation; the graphic is cryptic. The graphic could be made more useful by having buttons which provide explanation of each bar in pop-up windows.

DISTORTION OF   Some graphics distort the truth, and the distortion is
THE TRUTH   sometimes deliberate. Anyone interested in this sub-
                      ject should read the entertaining book *How to Lie
with Statistics* [5].

Often, the distortion is inadvertent—such as that caused by a graphic designer trained in art but not statistics. An author should know the ways in which graphics can distort the truth and avoid them, as follows.

Do Not Vary the Scale Intervals

One would not expect the U.S. National Science Foundation to distort the truth about American Nobel Prize winners, but look at Fig. 13.7[6].

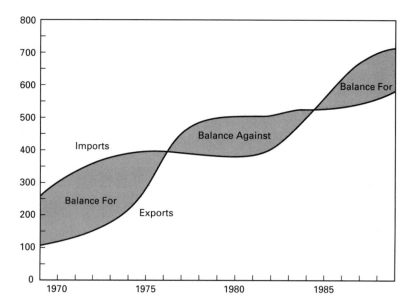

Figure 13.6 Most software which plots charts from numbers cannot draw the useful shading shown here.

It may surprise the reader to know that the number of Nobel Prizes awarded in science to the United States went *up* strongly in the 1970s, not *down* as Fig. 13.7 might suggest. Figure 13.8 shows the situation *less* misleadingly.

If you read the horizontal axis very carefully, Fig. 13.7 says why the curves go down at the right. The divisions are each for a 10-year period except for the last division, which is for a 5-year period. The second chart avoids this distortion by plotting a 10-year period for every division. Less misleading would be to plot the figures for five-year periods.

The first rule for integrity in drawing graphs is:

Don't vary the scale intervals.

Do Not Distort the Scales

Graphical scales can be distorted in a variety of ingenious ways. One way is to draw pictures apparently showing visual perspective. In Fig. 13.9 Tufte shows an example from *The New York Times*[7].

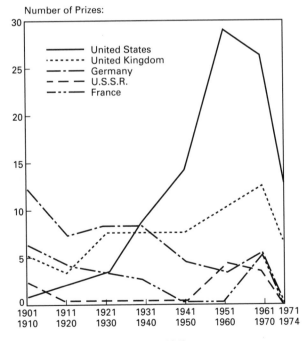

Figure 13.7

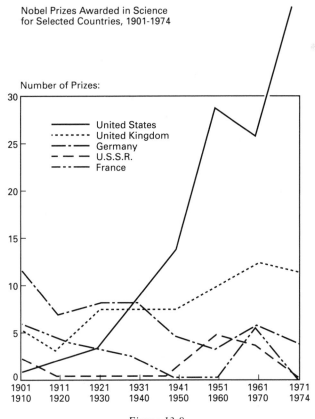

Figure 13.8

The change in fuel economy shown in this chart is 53 percent; the change in the line length representing fuel economy is 783 percent. The chart not only distorts the data, it hides an interesting fact: fuel economy is required to improve slowly to begin with, then change at a doubled rate from 1980 to 1983, then level off.

The second rule for integrity is:

Do not distort the scale of charts.

Start the Axes at Zero

A small difference in values can be made to appear impressive with a bar chart like that in Fig. 13.10.

The two charts in Fig. 13.11 disguise a serious decline in profitability. Al-

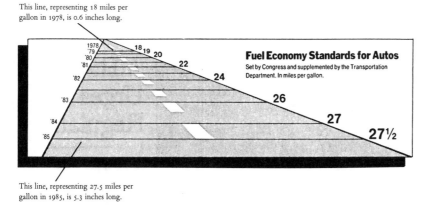

Figure 13.9 Copyright © 1978 by The New York Times Company. Reprinted by permission.

though the revenue is up by 4.6 percent, the profit is down by 14 percent—not what a casual glance at the charts would suggest.

The third rule for integrity is:

Start the graph axes at zero where practical.

Draw Variables as Lines, Not Objects

The chart from *Time* on the left hand side of Fig. 13.11 suggests an alarming increase in oil prices between 1974 and 1979[8]. The reader tends to equate the price increase with the volume of the barrel. The chart on the right of Fig 13.11 is less misleading.

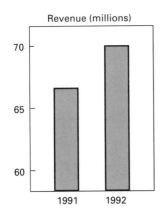
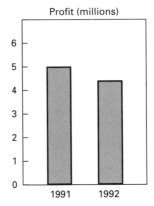

Figure 13.10

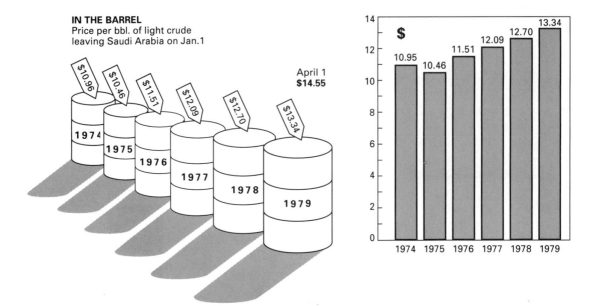

Figure 13.11   Oil prices. Compare the right-hand chart with that in Fig 13.12.
Copyright © 1979 Time Inc. Reprinted by permission.

The fourth rule for integrity is:

Draw variables as lines, not solids.

Show Money Adjusted for Inflation

From 1974 to 1979, there was substantial inflation. If oil prices are calculated in
1972 dollars, the price in 1978 is lower than 1974. As shown in Fig. 13.12, this
is different from the chart shown in Fig. 13.11.
    A further rule for integrity:

Show money values adjusted for inflation (as well as actual values).

Do Not Show Data Out of Context

In 1956, U.S. police imposed stricter enforcement of speed limits, and traffic
deaths declined. Figure 13.13 illustrates this[9].
    The decline in deaths could have had little to do with the police crack-
down. To see how one is related to the other, the figures for other years (Fig.
13.14) and other states (Fig. 13.15) should be shown.

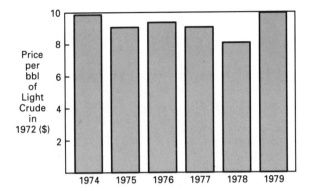

Figure 13.12   Oil prices, shown in Fig 13.11, adjusted for inflation.

From Figs. 13.14 and 13.15, it can be seen that Fig. 13.13 exaggerates the effect of the police activity.

Rule 6 is:

When charting cause and effect, do not take an isolated example out of context.

Where a chart contains possible causes for misunderstanding, clear comments should be added to avoid the misunderstanding.

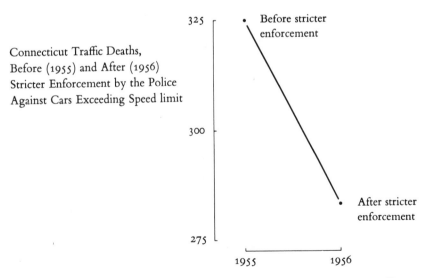

Figure 13.13   A misleading chart showing the effect of speed limit on traffic deaths. Compare with Fig 13.14[9].

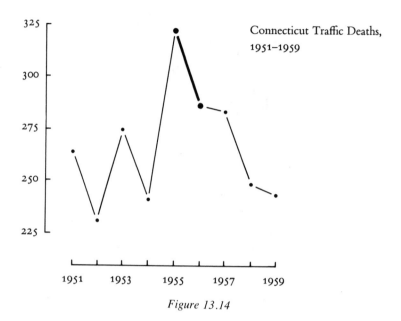

Figure 13.14

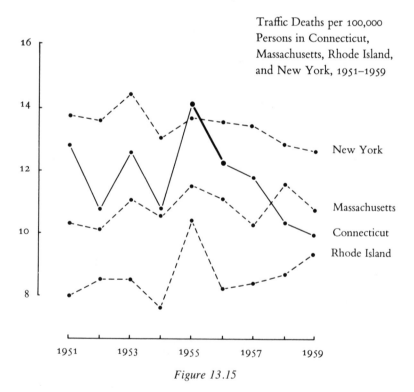

Figure 13.15

14 CHECKLIST OF STYLE RECOMMENDATIONS FOR DIAGRAMS

In a typical book, each chapter contains contiguous paragraphs of text. In a hyperdocument, a chapter may be a noncontiguous structure organized with envelopes, bullets, and buttons.

This chapter is a hierarchical list of bullets. The overall structure is as follows:

```
┌─ Checklist of style recommendations for diagrams

    . . . Overall structure
    . . . Elegant simplicity
    . . . Use of words
    . . . Use of color
    . . . Aesthetic considerations
└─  . . . Integrity
```

The rest of the chapter is an expansion of this structure.

```
┌─ Checklist of style recommendations for diagrams

   ┌─ Overall structure
```

FRIENDLY	UNFRIENDLY
• The diagram is self-explanatory.	• The diagram has insufficient explanation.
• Buttons are used to provide clear explanatory notes.	• Explanatory notes are not provided when needed.
• Most diagrams should occupy one screen and not need scrolling. An exception to this is charts with a very long scale.	• The diagram cannot be seen without scrolling.

(Continued)

FRIENDLY	UNFRIENDLY
• Highly complex diagrams are nested into separate diagrams each of which can be viewed on one screen where possible.	• At first glance the complexity appears daunting to the viewer.
• Lengthy lists are divided hierarchically, with usually no more than seven items in any one sublist.	
• There are no more than seven buttons on one diagram.	

Elegant simplicity

FRIENDLY	UNFRIENDLY
• The ratio of data pixels to nondata pixels is maximized, within reason.	
• Nondata pixels and redundant data pixels are eliminated, within reason.	
• The diagram is clean and uncluttered.	• Unnecessary decoration is used.
• Unneeded elaborations are avoided.	• Artwork is present other than the concise meaning of the chart.

Use of words

FRIENDLY	UNFRIENDLY
• The diagram has a self-explanatory caption.	• Caption is not self-explanatory.
	• Diagram has no caption.
• Acronyms are avoided.	• Acronyms abound.
• Graph axes are clearly labeled.	• Graph axes are unlabeled.
• Words are horizontal.	• Words are vertical.
• Diagram is labeled so that no key is required.	• Coding requires frequent examination of a key.
• Type is upper and lowercase, with serifs.	• Type is all capitals, sans

Use of color

FRIENDLY	UNFRIENDLY
• Colors are used to enhance comprehension.	• Colors are used for decoration without aiding comprehension.
	• Colors are not used.
• Colors are used so that most color-blind people can make sense of the graphic, by using strong contrasts and varying the shading.	• The design is insensitive to color-deficient viewers. (Blue cannot be distinguished from other colors by most color-deficient people.)

Aesthetic considerations

FRIENDLY	UNFRIENDLY
• The diagram attracts the viewer.	• The diagram is repellent.
• The diagram appears easy to understand.	• At first glance the diagram appears complex and difficult to understand.
• Bold and simple shadings on solid blocks are used.	• Elaborate shadings and cross-hatchings are used (which are so easy to create with compu-terized drawing tools).
• Lines of different thicknesses should be used to represent differences in meaning. The greater meaning is given to the thicker line.	
• The items on the diagram are arranged for maximum clarity. The diagram is well-balanced.	• The layout of the diagram is inelegant.
• The diagram is usually horiz-ontal rather than vertical. (Some diagrams are natural exceptions to this.)	

Integrity

CHARTS WITH INTEGRITY	MISLEADING CHARTS
• The axes of a graph start at zero.	• The axes of a graph do not start at zero. The chart may be designed so that the dif-ferences in values appear larger than they really are.
• The value on a bar chart is proportional to bar length.	• The value is proportional to width of a graphic which shows an area or volume, for example, a man, building, or oil barrel (see Fig. 13.11).
• The design does not vary across the chart. The scale interval does not vary.	• The axes change their scale in midchart.
• The scale is not distorted.	• The scale is distorted, for example by drawing it with apparent perspective.
• In time-series displays of money, show actual values and values adjusted for inflation.	• Time series displays of money do not show the effects of inflation.
• Data is not displayed out of context.	• Values are shown out of context to make a point.
• Any aspect of the figures which needs explaining is explained on the chart itself (or with a button on the chart).	• Ambiguities or anomalies are not explained.
• Clear and detailed labeling is used.	

PART **IV** MANAGEMENT CONSIDERATIONS

15 MAINTENANCE

LINK INTEGRITY A major reason for using hypertext documentation rather than paper is that information on computers can be updated easily. Any portion of a hyperdocument can be changed. Changes may be made by different people in different places.

While this is a major advantage of computerized information, it raises a big question: How can the integrity of hypertext be maintained when changes are being made? When a section of hypertext is changed, the links that point to that section need to be modified. These links may originate in other documents, possibly authored by other people in distant places. There may be complex relationships between different pieces of hypertext which are interlinked, and the pieces might change.

As with complex software, maintenance can be difficult (or near impossible) unless the hyperdocuments are carefully designed for maintenance. The design should minimize the difficulty of rebuilding the hypertext links when changes occur.

THREE MAINTENANCE PRINCIPLES Three principles apply to hypermedia maintenance.

First, when changes are made which require link modification, this modification should be done *automatically* by the software wherever possible. Hypertext authors should choose software which has the capability to rebuild the links automatically. They should know under what circumstances the software can do this and under what circumstances it cannot.

Second, when links cannot be rebuilt automatically, the software should inform the author what links he must rebuild manually.

Third, when some types of links cannot be rebuilt automatically, hypermedia authors should avoid the use of those links.

MAINTENANCE OF SINGLE-AUTHOR DOCUMENTS

We can consider two situations: first, documents with a single author and, second, documents with multiple authors.

After building many hypertext links, the author may still keep modifying his work. If he modifies something which is the target of a link, he may invalidate the link. He may delete the target, in which case the button and link to it should be deleted. He may reorganize the text so that the target is in a different envelope. In this case the link should be rebuilt so that it connects to the new location of the target.

In many cases, good hypertext software should be able to adjust the links automatically when the author makes changes, as follows:

Author Action:	Software Action:
Delete the button.	Delete the link.
Rename the button.	Modify the link.
Rename a word or phrase, all occurrences of which act as a button.	Modify all links which use those buttons.
Change location of the target.	Automatically modify all links which connect to that target using the new target.
Delete the target.	Delete the link and notify the author.
Completely restructure the target.	Detect the change when possible and ask the author if the link which connects to that target should be rebuilt.

CHOICE OF LINK TARGET

If any line of text is used as a link target, maintenance can become very difficult. The problem of managing dynamic change sometimes becomes uncontrollable. Maintenance is much easier if the targets of links are chosen with some basic rules.

A practical rule is to restrict the targets of Go-To links to the following:

- A glossary
- A concept unit
- An envelope (rather than detail within the envelope)
- A document

If the internals of these units are modified, the link will remain valid. If the location of the concept unit or diagram unit is changed, the links should be rebuilt *automatically* by the software.

Rules for making maintenance trouble-free should be known by the software. The software might enforce the rules or merely warn the author if he breaks the rules. A prudent author will not switch off the rule enforcement.

MAINTENANCE OF DOCUMENT INTEGRITY WITH MULTIPLE AUTHORS

Some documents are worked on by multiple authors. It is possible that one author may change the document so as to require the modification of links built by another author. If there is only one copy of the document, the preceding software actions should enable the change to take place. When multiple authors currently have copies of the document, changes can be controlled automatically only when the copies are under the control of one system.

When there are multiple copies of documents, change control presents a problem if hypertext links span multiple documents. It is generally desirable that links spanning documents be relatively simple in nature. They might be confined to the following categories:

- A link to a central glossary
- A link to a central collection of concept units
- A link to a central collection of diagrams
- A link to a document itself rather than to detail within the document

An organization employing multiple writers may have a central glossary and a central collection of concept units and diagram units which all authors share. Many hyperdocuments may have links to this centralized resource. The units in the centralized resource should be designed to be as stable as possible. The target of the links should be the unit as a whole, not some detail inside the unit.

INTERDOCUMENT LINKS

Sometimes a hypermedia link points to a different document. All interdocument links should point to a target document itself, not to details inside the document. The document may then be modified without invalidating the links which point to it.

16 ORGANIZING TEAMS OF AUTHORS

COORDINATION   Large bodies of documentation are likely to be worked on by teams of authors. Publishers of technical literature in hyperdocument form employ multiple authors, sometimes at scattered locations. Teams of authors require central coordination and appropriate software. There may be a central editor, separate from the coordinator, who helps improve the authors' English, style, and use of the medium.

An objective of the organization ought to be to maximize the productivity of the authors. The creation of hyperdocuments may be greatly speeded up by the use of centrally coordinated material to which all authors can hyperlink. It might also be helped by the use of a central artist, perhaps with a high-resolution scanner, who is skilled with a computerized drawing tool and perhaps an animation tool. The artist may have a collection of centrally maintained drawings and artwork.

CENTRAL RESOURCES   When the work of multiple authors is coordinated, the authors should share the following resources:

- A central glossary explaining technical terms.

- A central acronym list.

- A central (and growing) collection of concept units, each of which is stand-alone and self-contained and can be linked to (from many different documents). Each item in the glossary is a possible candidate for a tutorial explanation in a concept unit.

- A central (and growing) collection of diagrams, each of which is self-contained and clearly captioned.

- A central index of concept units.

- A central index of diagrams.
- A collection of templates which help in the design of documents and which help achieve consistency.

Each author should have a copy of this centrally maintained collection of resources (Fig. 16.1) available on his personal computer.

If an author is writing, for example, a detailed description of a new product using artificial intelligence techniques, he should not have to explain "forward chaining," "Rete algorithm," "inference engine," and so on; these terms are already described in the glossary or concept units, and the software should automatically build hyperlinks to the descriptions.

As the central collection of concept units and diagrams grows, so the productivity of the authors increases. They reuse what is already written.

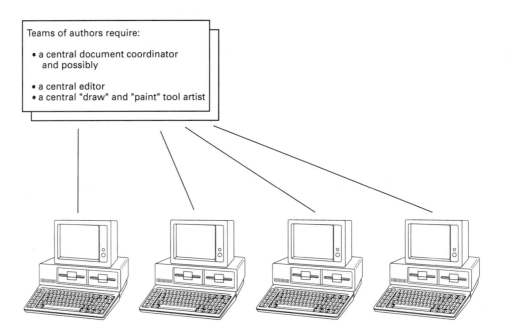

Teams of authors require:

- a central document coordinator
  and possibly

- a central editor
- a central "draw" and "paint" tool artist

Each author has access to (or has a copy of) a centrally maintained:

- glossary
- acronym list
- collection of concept units
- collection of diagrams, animation, etc.
- index of concept units
- index of diagrams

Figure 16.1 Facilities for teams of authors.

AVOIDANCE OF COMMITTEES

Almost all good writing is produced by one individual. For that matter almost all true creativity stems from one individual. Management should give the creative individual as much support as possible without impeding his creativity.

When we talk about managing teams of authors we are not suggesting that writing should be done by a committee. Committees can criticize; they cannot create:

> Search the parks in all your cities;
> You'll find no statues of committees.

When committees produce documents they are invariably a patchwork of the views of different individuals, most of whom hide in committees because they cannot create good work alone. Creative individuals have a knack of avoiding committees. Some of the world's worst writing is that done by committees.

Committees not only produce camels which were intended to be racehorses, they take an unreasonably large number of person-hours in doing so. A competent author can write a thousand words per day. Two authors working together are likely to average half of that—a quarter of the productivity. Three authors are likely to produce a third—one-ninth of the productivity.

To manage teams of authors, then, give each writer the job of producing a discrete document by himself. Set guidelines about style and use of central resources such as a glossary, concept units, art facilities, and templates. Work out in advance how different documents should link together and what common templates should be used. Use meetings for brainstorming and fact-finding, but not for the actual writing.

CREATIVITY AND FREEDOM

We want hyperdocument authors to be as creative as possible. Hypermedia are so rich in creative potential.

Creativity does not imply an absence of order. The writer should operate with tools and guidelines which are known to work well. David Ogilvy ran an advertising agency renowned for creativity. It grew to become one of the world's largest agencies. Ogilvy developed 96 factors which were shown in the marketplace to make advertisements succeed. The creative copywriters had to operate within this codified experience. Ogilvy criticized less successful agencies for failing to measure and codify what factors made creativity successful in selling. He commented: "If you choose to ignore these factors, good luck to you. A blind pig can sometimes find truffles, but it helps to know that they are found in oak forests."[1]

Creativity and freedom are most valuable within a well-managed framework. The creative author needs to be provided with resources which aid his creativity. In the world of hyperdocuments these resources become complex. They need standards. Cicero stated: "We are in bondage to the law in order that we may be free."

Creativity does not imply a Bohemian artist in garret. It implies a management style which provides the resources, guidelines, encouragement, and rewards for individualism. Valuable creativity can be the fruit of well-organized management.

SOFTWARE

The software for creating hyperdocuments should facilitate central coordination and provide as much help as possible in increasing author productivity. Characteristics of the software should be as follows:

- A central glossary, acronym list, and collection of concept units and diagrams should be available to each author.
- There should be an index of concept units and diagrams.
- The envelopes on the author's screen should make it clear which are concept units and which are diagrams.
- The software should be able to scan the authors' text and automatically build buttons to the glossary and concept units.
- The software should aid in maintenance of hyperdocuments by automatically rebuilding hyperlinks when items are moved (and generally providing the facilities discussed in Chapter 15).
- The authors should use a common diagramming tool with "paint" and "draw" capabilities.
- The authors may use a common, numeric charting tool.
- The authors may use common software for diagram animation.
- A central document scanner may be available to the authors.
- The authors may use a common word processor or electronic publishing package.
- A spelling checker should be available, possibly on a word processor separate from the primary authoring software.
- Software may apply checks to the author's grammar.
- Software may check that the author obeys style guidelines such as maximum length of envelopes and paragraphs.
- There may be a set of document templates which the authors can use, expand, and modify.

CENTRAL COORDINATION OF HYPERDOCUMENT AUTHORS

It is necessary to coordinate the work of multiple hyperdocument authors under one person. This person is concerned with the quality and consistency of their work and with maximizing their productivity by the employment of central resources.

The document coordinator has three categories of tasks:

- Maintain the central glossary, concept units, and other resources.

- Provide services to the authors (such as a scanner service and graphics artist).

- Communicate with the authors, ensuring that they understand the working methodology.

- Perform copy editing.

- Check the authors' work for quality and consistency, editing it where appropriate.

- Link the work of different authors into an overall structure.

These tasks are expanded in more detail in Fig. 16.2.

CENTRAL CONCEPT UNITS AND DEFINITIONS

The more complete the central glossary and collection of concept units, the less the work the authors have to do. The document coordinator should help build this central repository. Authors frequently create new concept units or glossary definitions. These should be added to the central repository. Sometimes an author will feel the need to improve a glossary item or concept unit. This improvement should be made, providing there is no disagreement from other authors. When disagreements occur, a hyperdocument coordinator must eventually resolve the disagreement.

The coordinator acts rather like a data administrator for information systems development, ensuring that there is agreement about definitions of items and ensuring that the concept units are correctly "normalized," that is, standalone and independent of the subject of the document which links to them.

CENTRAL DIAGRAMS

A central collection of diagrams may be maintained, which can be used by authors working on different types of documents. An author requiring a diagram may do one of four things:

- Use an existing diagram, possibly changing the words on it.

- Modify an existing diagram.

- Create a new diagram.

- Have a control artist create the diagram.

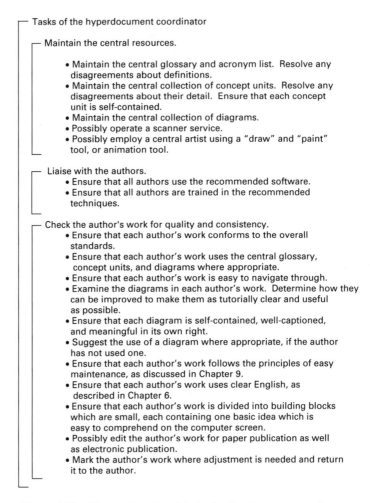

Tasks of the hyperdocument coordinator

Maintain the central resources.

- Maintain the central glossary and acronym list. Resolve any disagreements about definitions.
- Maintain the central collection of concept units. Resolve any disagreements about their detail. Ensure that each concept unit is self-contained.
- Maintain the central collection of diagrams.
- Possibly operate a scanner service.
- Possibly employ a central artist using a "draw" and "paint" tool, or animation tool.

Liaise with the authors.
- Ensure that all authors use the recommended software.
- Ensure that all authors are trained in the recommended techniques.

Check the author's work for quality and consistency.
- Ensure that each author's work conforms to the overall standards.
- Ensure that each author's work uses the central glossary, concept units, and diagrams where appropriate.
- Ensure that each author's work is easy to navigate through.
- Examine the diagrams in each author's work. Determine how they can be improved to make them as tutorially clear and useful as possible.
- Ensure that each diagram is self-contained, well-captioned, and meaningful in its own right.
- Suggest the use of a diagram where appropriate, if the author has not used one.
- Ensure that each author's work follows the principles of easy maintenance, as discussed in Chapter 9.
- Ensure that each author's work uses clear English, as described in Chapter 6.
- Ensure that each author's work is divided into building blocks which are small, each containing one basic idea which is easy to comprehend on the computer screen.
- Possibly edit the author's work for paper publication as well as electronic publication.
- Mark the author's work where adjustment is needed and return it to the author.

Figure 16.2   Three categories of tasks for the document coordinator.

Because diagrams are so important to tutorial clarity and so effective in hyperdocuments, a coordinating editor may suggest to an author that he use a diagram in places where he has not used one. An artist who is skilled at creating computerized diagrams or animation may be employed centrally to help the authors. He may have created many of the central collection of diagrams and can modify them quickly.

The coordinating editor should ensure that each diagram is self-contained and well captioned so that it is meaningful in its own right, no matter what the reader has seen prior to examining the diagram.

EDITING THE AUTHORS' WORK   Most publishing organizations employ an editor to improve the authors' English. A publisher of electronic documents should be concerned not only with English (or Japanese, French, German, etc.) but with the other characteristics described in this work which constitute good style in hyperdocuments. The editor may modify the author's English, diagrams, or structuring or may request that the author modify them. It is usually efficient for the editor to make minor changes and request that the author make the major changes. A copy editor may run the author's work through a spelling checker and, possibly, use software which checks for misuses of grammar.

The software should make it clear to the author what the editor has changed (for example, the changes could be in a different color) and should provide a mechanism which the editor can use to leave electronic notes in the document for the author. The editor may make changes by duplicating an author's line in a different color (immediately below the original line) and modifying the duplicate line. The software should enable the editor to accomplish this rapidly.

MAINTENANCE   Even when there is only one author, care needs to be taken that hyperdocuments are built so that they can be maintained easily. When there are multiple authors, possibly in different locations, this concern is even more important. The central coordinator must be concerned with the issues discussed in Chapter 14, which help achieve maintainability. Software must be selected which aids the maintenance process.

Teams of authors require

- A central document coordinator (see Fig. 16.2) and, possibly,
- A central editor
- A central "draw" and "paint" tool artist

Each author has access to a copy of centrally maintained

- Glossary
- Acronym list
- Collection of concept units
- Collection of diagrams, animation, and so on
- An index of concept units
- An index of diagrams

AN ORGANIZATION WHICH CREATES TECHNICAL REPORTS

Consider an organization which creates technical reports to review complex products and explain what they do. The organization publishes many volumes, each on a different subject and each containing many articles which may be written by different authors.

THE PLAYERS

Separate well-structured documents provide different approaches to the same subject matter, the different approaches being designed to solve the problems of people with different needs. Charts are used showing the strengths and weaknesses of products, functionality of products, or how products relate to issues or problems. The charts, and editorial comments, lead the reader to more indepth technical details.

For each volume there is a *volume editor* who is an expert on the subject matter of the volume. There is also an *editor-in-chief* who is familiar with all the volumes. A *copy editor,* who is not an expert on the subject matter, helps all authors to use good English. (See Fig. 16.3.)

The volume editor is responsible for the articles and hyperlinks within his volume. He will create the organizing structure for the volume and liaise with the authors. The volume editor updates the glossary entries, concept units, diagrams, and templates for his area of expertise.

The editor-in-chief is responsible for the entire series of volumes, creating the organizing structure for the series and acting as liaison with the volume editors. He will build hyperlinks which span volumes and link them to the introductory volume. The editor-in-chief has final responsibility for the glossary and central collection of concept units and templates, resolving any disputes about details of glossary definitions and concept units.

When an author has created a document, it goes to the volume editor. The volume editor knows how this product relates to other products, and so fits the document into the organizing structure of the volume. The templates provided to the authors ensure that the individual documents blend well with the rest of the volume. The volume editor hyperlinks the piece into his overall structure, his editorial, charts of product comparisons, and so on.

A new article may bring new insights, in which case the volume editor may modify his introduction to the volume or the charts which organize the volume. He rebuilds the volume links if necessary.

The volume editor sends the completed volume to the editor-in-chief. The editor-in-chief knows how to cross-link the ideas in this volume to those in other volumes and to the material which introduces and organizes the volume series.

For example, if the series is about computer software, there might be separate volumes on fourth-generation languages, code generators, artificial intelligence, and database systems. A reader might be concerned about when he should use a fourth-generation language and when a code generator, hence there need to be links connecting these volumes. Database systems employ fourth-

Author
The authors write articles on specified subjects in hyperdocument
form.

Responsibilities
- Research the subject.
- Organize the material into structures which make it as clear
  as possible.
- Devise the clearest possible diagrams.
- Create the diagrams, possibly using a central artist or
  scanning service.
- Build buttons on the diagrams.
  - Write text as concisely and clearly as possible.
- Build hyperlinks within the article.
- Build hyperlinks to centralized glossary items and concept
  units.
- Build intelligence into the article, as described in Chapter 8,
  if appropriate.
- Possibly create both a paper version and an electronic version
  of the article.

Copy Editor
The Copy Editor does not understand the subject matter but helps
all authors to use clear English and to create good hyperdocument
structures.

Responsibilities
- Correct the author's spelling and grammar.
- Edit the work to give it an attractive and consistent screen
  appearance.
- Ensure that each author's work uses clear English, as
  described in Chapter 6.
- Ensure that each author's work is divided into idea units
  which are short, each containing one basic idea which is
  easy to comprehend on the computer screen.
- Ensure that each diagram is self-contained, well-captioned,
  and meaningful in its own right.
- Examine the diagrams in each author's work. Determine how they
  can be improved to make them as tutorially clear and useful
  as possible.
- Suggest the use of a diagram where appropriate, if the author
  has not used one.
- Mark the author's work where adjustment is needed and return
  it to the author.
- Possibly edit the author's work for paper publication as well
  as electronic publication.

Volume Editor
The Volume Editor is an expert on the subject matter of a volume.
He works with the authors who create articles for the volume.
He may author some of the material himself.

Responsibilities
Liaise with the authors.
- Ensure that all authors use the recommended software,
  glossary, concept units, etc.
- Ensure that all authors are familiar with the recommended
  techniques.

Figure 16.3 Tasks of authors, volume editors, copy editor, and editor-in-chief. (This chart is an expanded printout from a hyperdocument, the reader of which would see the envelope titles first, before expanding them.)

(Continued)

Check the author's work for quality and consistency.
- Ensure that each author's work conforms to the overall standards.
- Ensure that each author's work uses the central glossary, concept units and diagrams where appropriate.
- Ensure that each author's work is easy to navigate through.
- Examine the diagrams in each author's work. Determine how they can be improved to make them tutorially clear and useful as possible.
- Suggest the use of a diagram where appropriate if the author has not used one.
- Ensure that each author's work follows the principles of easy maintenance, discussed in Chapter 9.
- Mark the author's work where adjustment is needed and return it to the author.

Create volume-specific material.
- Devise how the volume is organized, possibly creating a diagram to show the organization.
- Build the volume Table of Contents.
- Create the front matter.
- Write an editorial and overall introduction.
- Create templates for categorizing the features in the products which are reviewed.

Build hyperlinks within the volume.
- Link the articles to the Table of Contents.
- Link the articles to the editorial, introduction, and diagrams showing the volume organization.
- Link the articles to lists of issues.
- Link the articles to charts which categorize the products.
- Build links between articles where appropriate.

Editor-in-Chief
The Editor-in-Chief is responsible for all volumes, and for the centralized resources which the authors employ.

Responsibilities
Create volume-independent material.
- Devise how the series of volumes is organized, possibly creating a diagram to show the organization.
- Build a Table of Contents for the entire series of volumes.
- Create introductory material to the series of volumes.
- Determine what templates can help achieve consistency among the volumes.

Maintain the central resources.
- Maintain the central glossary and acronym list. Resolve any disagreements about definitions.
- Maintain the central collection of concept units. Resolve any disagreements about their detail. Ensure that each concept unit is self-contained.
- Maintain the central collection of diagrams.
- Maintain the central collection of templates which guide the authors and volume editors.
- Maintain standards to achieve consistency.

Figure 16.3   (Continued)

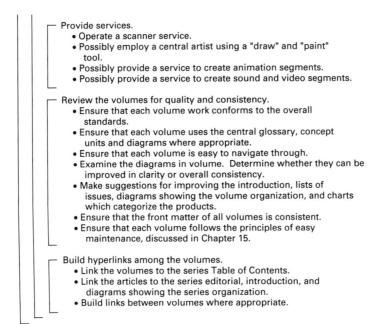

Provide services.
- Operate a scanner service.
- Possibly employ a central artist using a "draw" and "paint" tool.
- Possibly provide a service to create animation segments.
- Possibly provide a service to create sound and video segments.

Review the volumes for quality and consistency.
- Ensure that each volume work conforms to the overall standards.
- Ensure that each volume uses the central glossary, concept units and diagrams where appropriate.
- Ensure that each volume is easy to navigate through.
- Examine the diagrams in volume. Determine whether they can be improved in clarity or overall consistency.
- Make suggestions for improving the introduction, lists of issues, diagrams showing the volume organization, and charts which categorize the products.
- Ensure that the front matter of all volumes is consistent.
- Ensure that each volume follows the principles of easy maintenance, discussed in Chapter 15.

Build hyperlinks among the volumes.
- Link the volumes to the series Table of Contents.
- Link the articles to the series editorial, introduction, and diagrams showing the series organization.
- Build links between volumes where appropriate.

Figure 16.3   (Continued)

generation languages; hence these volumes are linked. An expert in artificial intelligence might read the review of a mainframe tool for building expert systems, and be bewildered by references to IMS, a database system, and so he follows a hyperlink into the database volume which explains IMS.

The introduction to the series of volumes explores and illuminates the relationships among fourth-generation languages, code generators, artificial intelligence, and database systems and links to the appropriate envelopes in these volumes.

Some hyperdocuments might use expert-system techniques. For example, a rule-based system might be used to perform a needs analysis for the selection of application development software. Figure 16.4 illustrates how this rule-based system might lead the reader to segments of other volumes which can help with his problems.

The products being reviewed change rapidly, so the entire set of volumes is in flux. Although the products change, the concept units should be designed so that they rarely need to be modified. The volume editors and editor-in-chief must design the structures to facilitate maintenance of hyperlinks which could become difficult to maintain. Different types of multiauthor teams have organizations which are different from this, but the same general principles apply.

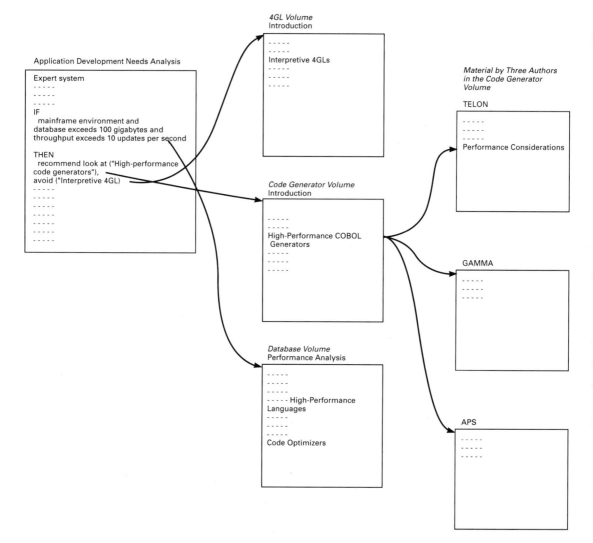

Figure 16.4 How a rule-based system helps lead readers to segments of interest in related volumes.

CONVERTING HYPERDOCUMENTS TO PRINTED DOCUMENTS

Organizations which create hyperdocuments sometimes want a paper document containing the same information. The paper document will not be identical to the electronic document because the paper document does not have hyperlinks and may need to use brackets slightly differently. To take an author's hyperdocument and make a good paper document of it is a straightforward editing task. The copy editor may be given this task.

It is desirable that the contents of the hyperdocument should be directly convertible into a form which can be handled by electronic publishing software. The editing for print should take place in the electronic publishing software.

THE PRODUCTION PROCESS

The editor-in-chief, working with the volume editors, determines what volumes are required and who will produce them. He creates the overall organizing structure for the series of volumes. He creates templates which aid the volume editor, and the volume editor provides the authors with templates.

The author creates a hyperdocument, using software which automatically builds links to the glossary and collection of concept units. The author may create new glossary entries and new concept units. These are approved by the volume editor and passed to the editor-in-chief for incorporation in the central repository. If there are disagreements about the details of the glossary definitions or concept units, the editor-in-chief has the final responsibility for resolving these.

17 CONVERTING PAPER DOCUMENTS TO HYPERDOCUMENTS

THE NEED TO CONVERT PAPER DOCUMENTS
The world is full of large paper documents which ought to be on computer disks. These large collections of paper—maintenance manuals, regulations, machine manuals, software manuals, libraries of reports, government documents, accountants' procedures, encyclopedias, methodology documents, and so on—are rapidly becoming anachronisms, soon to go the way of the buffalo.

It is relatively easy to convert this mass of paper to CD-ROMs. A computer can build indices far more thorough than paper indices and the CD-ROMs can be searched at high speed. However, it is desirable to do more than dump the documents onto CDs; we ought to build links so that they become hyperdocuments.

Some hyperlinks can be built automatically, for example, links to a glossary or acronym list. A collection of concept units may be built for the subject matter and automatically linked to it. A hierarchical table of contents will be built for the subject matter. Possibly libraries of documents will be hyperlinked to a unifying structure.

The result of this may still violate most of the principles of good hyperdocuments described in this book. Much manual effort is needed to convert existing paper into *quality* hyperdocuments. Some organizations have done this and have commented that a large amount of work is needed.

The conversion process is somewhat analogous to the task of converting old data processing programs, which are often ill-structured, into well-structured programs which can take advantage of modern databases. The term "reverse engineering" is used for this. Some old programs are not worth converting; some are readily convertible; some are best scrapped and rewritten. The same is true with converting documents. Some documents are sow's ears and it will be a frustrating task to turn them into silk purses.

THE CONVERSION AUTHORS

To create high-quality hyperdocuments from paper documents usually needs some rewriting. This may be cosmetic changes, it may be restructuring which needs minor rewriting, or it may be reauthoring to split segments or create concept units. The diagrams may be improved with computer graphics tools. New charts may be created to summarize items in the document or help the reader to navigate.

Because some rewriting is usually necessary, it is appropriate to refer to persons who do such conversion as "conversion authors." It would help if one of the original authors was on the conversion team.

Sometimes people skilled at hyperdocument techniques can create better hyperdocuments than the original authors, just as a conductor is usually better than a composer at conducting the composer's work. There is therefore a major opportunity for service firms to offer a document conversion service.

CONVERSION OF A MAJOR ENCYCLOPEDIA

The *Engineering Data Compendium* [1], a four-volume, 3000-page encyclopedia, was converted to a CD-ROM hyperdocument [2]. This is a scientific and engineering encyclopedia that contains comprehensive reference data about human perception and performance. It is intended for people who design systems with complex human-machine interfaces, such as power plant control rooms, battle control stations on board ships, and aircraft cockpits.

The CD-ROM is being linked to the U.S. Air Force *Designer's Associate* [3]. This uses artificial intelligence techniques to help designers formulate questions and find relevant information about the design of systems with complex human interfaces. There is thus a valuable combination of artificial intelligence and hyperdocument techniques.

The complete text of the *Engineering Data Compendium* occupies about 15M bytes. The graphics are all bit mapped and required another 150M bytes. Extensive compression of these was needed for timely retrieval and display. Another 150M bytes was needed for various indices. It is difficult to imagine a paper document with indices ten times longer than the text! The CD-ROM thus contains about 315M bytes, so much of its 650M-bytes capacity is empty.

To speed up access on the personal computer, when text is read that has an associated graphic that graphic is read into a main memory "cache." Text entries for the next and previous entries of the table of contents are also cached.

The *Engineering Data Compendium* is concerned with human perception, sensation, and performance. It contains much detail from experiments, research, and predictive models, represented in tables and graphs. There is discussion of principles and background information to help users understand and evaluate the data.

The encyclopedia is segmented into 1138 entries, each of which is self-contained and deals with a narrow, well-defined topic. Each topic entry has two or more figures which show the key findings graphically. There are about 2000 illustrations in total. Each topic entry contains all or more of the following parts:

- Title
- Key terms
- General description
- Applications
- Methods
- Experiment results
- Empirical validation
- Constraints
- Key references
- Cross-references
- Figure/table captions

The encyclopedia thus fits well the structure we have described with envelopes, brackets, concept units, and glossary entries. Its Index has about 2000 top-level headings and 10,000 entries. There is a composite *Index of Key Terms,* equivalent to the index of concept units we have described. In addition, there is a *Design Checklist* and a set of *Design Questions.* These form an application-oriented hierarchical navigation structure for the user, which is quite separate from the hierarchical taxonomy of the table of contents. At the lowest level in this application-oriented hierarchy there are questions which the designer might ask about human perception and performance. These questions link to the relevant topic entries (Fig. 8.4).

**STEPS IN THE
CONVERSION**

Figure 17.1 lists possible steps in the conversion process.

**CONVERSION
TO COMPUTER-
PROCESSABLE
FORM**

Once the decision has been made to computerize a paper document, the first step is to convert it to a machine-processable form. This may be easy when a word processor version exists of the original and the diagrams can be easily scanned. Sometimes there are problems, for example, translating obscure typesetting codes. Sometimes documents have to be rekeyed into a computer.

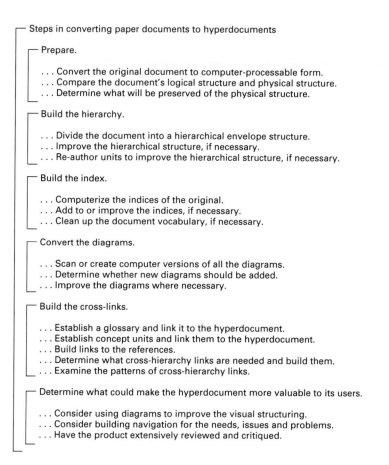

Steps in converting paper documents to hyperdocuments

Prepare.

. . . Convert the original document to computer-processable form.
. . . Compare the document's logical structure and physical structure.
. . . Determine what will be preserved of the physical structure.

Build the hierarchy.

. . . Divide the document into a hierarchical envelope structure.
. . . Improve the hierarchical structure, if necessary.
. . . Re-author units to improve the hierarchical structure, if necessary.

Build the index.

. . . Computerize the indices of the original.
. . . Add to or improve the indices, if necessary.
. . . Clean up the document vocabulary, if necessary.

Convert the diagrams.

. . . Scan or create computer versions of all the diagrams.
. . . Determine whether new diagrams should be added.
. . . Improve the diagrams where necessary.

Build the cross-links.

. . . Establish a glossary and link it to the hyperdocument.
. . . Establish concept units and link them to the hyperdocument.
. . . Build links to the references.
. . . Determine what cross-hierarchy links are needed and build them.
. . . Examine the patterns of cross-hierarchy links.

Determine what could make the hyperdocument more valuable to its users.

. . . Consider using diagrams to improve the visual structuring.
. . . Consider building navigation for the needs, issues and problems.
. . . Have the product extensively reviewed and critiqued.

Figure 17.1   Steps in the conversion process.

COMPARING PHYSICAL AND LOGICAL STRUCTURES

The logical structure of the document must be compared with the physical structure. The physical structure refers to page layout, line lengths, typographical conventions, margin headings, and other aspects of the document's appearance. *Logical structure* refers to the hierarchical arrangement of segments of text, how diagrams link to text, the table of contents and index, numbering scheme, references, cross-references, and any special devices for giving structure. Physical aspects such as fonts, spacing, or layout might have been used by the original authors to signal *logical* structure in the text.

The designers of the electronic document need to decide how closely the computer version will preserve the physical structure of the paper version. Will fonts be used in the same way? How will the diagrams be converted? A personal computer screen does not have as high a resolution as a book page. Will scanning the diagrams make them look good on the computer screen? Should the diagrams be enhanced, by color, better drawing, good use of buttons, animation, linkage of graphs and tables, and so on? The challenge is to use the computer screen to add features that the paper version does not have. Sometimes the conversion authors add more illustrative charts, checklists, and pictures.

BUILDING AN ENVELOPE HIERARCHY

The next step is to build a hierarchical structure for the document, putting its contents into hierarchical envelopes and using software which makes navigation through the hierarchy fast and easy. First, the hierarchy in the original document should be used; then, the conversion authors should decide whether this hierarchy needs improving. It may be useful to segment parts of the text which was not segmented in the original. Where segments contain more than one topic, minor rewriting may be needed to achieve a better structure.

The conversion authors should examine the overall structure in the contractable brackets, and decide whether it can be improved.

BUILDING INDICES AND GLOSSARY

The index of the original document should be computerized. Software may be available to build an index automatically. It should be decided what terms should be in a glossary. Existing glossary items may be used if they are available. A glossary file should be created and automatically hyperlinked to the document.

CONCEPT UNITS

When the glossary has been linked, a manual pass should be made through the document checking its vocabulary. Sometimes alternate or confusing terms are used. The software can take every instance of a word and change it to an alternate word. The vocabulary and glossary links should be cleaned up, if necessary.

As this is done, a list should be made of potential concept units. A concept unit, as discussed in Chapter 5, should provide a brief tutorial on a basic concept. They may be links from all parts of the document to a central collection of concept units. The conversion authors should decide what concept units are needed and build them, taking the text from the original document, where possible, and writing new text of this seems necessary. The concept units can be automatically hyperlinked to the text.

If the paper document does not have names for the lowest-level units, the conversion authors should create helpful names for the head of the envelope brackets.

LITERATURE REFERENCES

Each reference in the text to literature should be linked to the details of that item.

BUILDING THE DIAGRAMS

The diagrams in the original may be scanned, expanded, shrunk, or edited to make them display well and fit in with the text.

The convertors of the *Engineering Data Compendium* could not display on the screen of the personal computer both a diagram and the associated text. They enabled their readers to toggle from one to the other. Sometimes the screen could not show both a diagram and its caption. The caption was therefore put into a flat scrollable window.

In some cases, new diagrams should be created with graphics software. This may be done to improve the appearance of the original and add color to them. It may be done to create new charts, summaries, or diagrams of document structure. Sometimes the paper document is verbose and tedious to read on the computer screen. The lengthy wording may be replaceable with charts and a more visual presentation (like the charts used in a well-constructed lecture).

BUILDING CROSS-HIERARCHY LINKS

It should be determined what links spanning hierarchies will be useful. It is desirable not to create links merely because they are possible, but rather to create them in order to have a specific usefulness to the reader. A conversion author, like an original author, should have reader firmly in mind, and think about his problems and how to help solve them.

When many links have been built, it is useful if the authoring software can produce a summary of the links.

A useful way to view the links which are not part of hierarchies is with a square matrix whose rows and columns are the envelope names. The cells in the matrix show the number of links connecting two envelopes (including higher-level envelopes). This matrix is not symmetric because many links are unidirectional. Such a matrix shows the patterns of interactions. The conversion authors may judge whether the patterns have an appropriate sense of proportion. In converting the *Engineering Data Compendium* it was found that there were an abnormally high number of cross-references from entries in the "Display Interfaces" topic to those in the "Vision" topic, but there were few in the opposite direction. It was established that the reason for this was that the "Vision" entries were written first. Conversion authors might want to address an imbalance like this and build links in the opposite direction.

BUILDING NAVIGATION AIDS

The conversion authors should think about what techniques they can use to help the readers find the document as useful as possible. They may build visual aids to navigation. They may create a hierarchy which relates to the readers' problems, needs, and issues and link this alternate front end to the relevant segments of the document.

REVIEW AND CRITICISM

The new hyperdocument should be reviewed by multiple users with different needs and skill levels. It should be critiqued thoroughly, and the conversion authors should spend considerable time polishing and improving the hyperdocument, based on the user responses.

TO WHAT EXTENT CAN CONVERSION BE AUTOMATED?

Software can provide much assistance in converting paper documents to hyperdocuments. Figure 17.2 lists software features which help with the conversion. There has been discussion of automated conversion. However, good quality conversion is likely to need the human skills in authoring and devising clear structures. "Reverse engineering" of documents in a largely automated fashion would often result in documents which are tedious and less useful than they should be.

The conversion of the *Engineering Data Compendium* from paper to hyperdocument worked well because the original was well structured and well thought out. Many paper documents are ill structured and muddled. When one tries to convert them one realizes how muddled they are. If their authors had written them with the tools described in this book they would have been much better documents.

Even muddled documents are usually structured hierarchically. They have chapters, sections, and subsections. These can be put into hierarchical envelopes with bracket diagrams so that the reader can navigate through the hierarchy at high speed. Usually the text can be read into the hyperdocument tool automatically. Indices can be built automatically, and the diagrams can be scanned for computer display.

Beyond that, the person responsible for the conversion has a decision: How much work should be put into improving the document, separating its ideas into discrete units, reorganizing it, building hyperlinks, and possibly building alternate navigation hierarchies. Some people with an editor's mentality like doing this type of work; other people hate it. A judgment needs to be made about whether restructuring is worth it. How difficult would it be? Does it sufficiently increase the *value* of the document?

Functions in the hyperdocument authoring software.

Automatically build a hierarchical envelope structure.
Documents which use a hierarchical numbering scheme for numbering segments can be converted automatically to a hierarchical envelope structure, with a bracket diagram.

Computerize the indices of the original.
A computerized index can be built, based on the words indexed in the original.

Replace words automatically.
Scan for all occurrences of a word and replace it with a different word (to help in cleaning up the vocabulary).

Automatically build hyperlinks to an existing glossary.
When a glossary exists hyperlinks can be built to it automatically.

Automatically build hyperlinks to concept units.
When concept units have been established, hyperlinks can be built to them automatically.

Build other hyperlinks automatically, where possible.
For example, part numbers may be automatically linked to part descriptions or drawings.

Automatically build links to the literature references.
If the literature references have a standard numbering scheme, links can be built automatically from the numbers in the text to the list of references.

Analyze the patterns of cross-hierarchy links.
Produce a summary report of the hyperlinks, possibly in the form of a matrix, so that the overall balance of the document can be examined.

Connections to other tools.

Convert the original document to computer-processable form.
There should be direct input from word-processing software to the hyperdocument authoring software.

Convert the hyperdocument to electronic publishing form.
There should be direct input from hyperdocument software to electronic publishing software.

Scan and edit the original diagrams.
A scanner with editing software should be used to capture the original diagrams, edit them, change their size, and make them fit in with the text.

Make use of graphics software.
Links to different graphics packages may be needed to create new diagrams, charts of numbers, and representations of the document structure. It should be possible to "snap" screens from various software packages and build buttons on the images.

Figure 17.2   Software features which help in conversion to hyperdocuments.

194

18 REFERENCES

Chapter 3

[1] Information from Herb Schorr of IBM, 1988.

Chapter 4

[1] Noel Coward's commentary is from *Noel Coward* by Gilbert Millstein, Dell Publishing, New York, 1955.

Chapter 5

[1] James Martin, *Telecommunications and the Computer*, 2nd ed., Prentice-Hall, Englewood Cliffs, NJ, 1976.
[2] James Martin, *Managing the Data-Base Environment*, Prentice-Hall, Englewood Cliffs, NJ, 1983.

Chapter 6

[1] David Ogilvy, *Ogilvy on Advertising*, Crown Books, New York, 1983.
[2] Edward R. Tufte, *The Visual Display of Quantitative Information*, Graphics Press, Cheshire, CT, 1983.

Chapter 8

[1] K. R. Boff and J. E. Lincoln, *Engineering Data Compendium: Human Perception and Performance*, AAMRL, Wright-Patterson Air Force Base, Dayton, OH, 1988.
[2] K. R. Boff, "The Tower of Babel Revisited: On Cross-Disciplinary Choke-points in System Design," in *System Design: Behavioral Perspectives on Designers, Tools and Organizations*, Elsevier, New York, 1987.

Chapter 9

[1] Rosser Reeves, *Reality in Advertising*, Alfred Knopf, New York, 1961.

Chapter 10

[1] G. A. Miller, "The Magical Number Seven, Plus or Minus Two: Some Limits on Our Capacity for Information Processing," *Psychological Review*, Vol. 63, No. 2 March 1956, pp. 81-97.

Chapter 11

[1] William Strunk, Jr., and E. B. White, *The Elements of Style*, 3rd ed., Mac-Millan, New York, 1979.
[2] Sir Ernest Gower, *The Complete Plain Words*, rev. S. Greenbaum and J. Witout, 3rd ed., Penguin, Harmondsworth, U.K., 1987.
[3] Samuel R. Roget, *Roger's Thesaurus*, Crown Publishers, New York, 1987.
[4] H. W. Fowler, *Modern English Usage*, rev. Sir Ernest Gower, New Ed., Oxford University Press, Oxford, 1968.
[5] Denis Higgins, ed., *The Art of Writing Advertising*, Advertising Publications, New York, 1957.
[6] Julian L. Watkins, *The 100 Greatest Advertisements (Who Wrote Them & What They Did*, Dover Publications, New York, 1959.
[7] Daniel Hillis, "The Connection Machine," Scientific American, May, 1987.
[8] T. S. Eliot, "The Function of Criticism," *Selected Essays 1917-1932*, New York, 1932.

Chapter 12

[1] T. S. Eliot, "The Function of Criticism," *Selected Essays 1917-1932*, New York, 1932.
[2] E. J. Marey, *La Methode Graphique*, Paris, 1885; quoted in Edward R. Tufte, *The Visual Display of Quantitative Information*, Graphics Press, Cheshire, CT, 1983.
[3] Edward R. Tufte, *The Visual Display of Quantitative Information*, Graphics Press, Cheshire, CT, 1983.
[4] Linus C. Pauling, *General Chemistry*, 3rd ed., W.H. Freeman and Company, New York, 1970.
[5] Mary Eleanor Spear, *Charting Statistics*, New York, 1952; quoted in Edward R. Tufte, *The Visual Display of Quantitative Information*, Graphics Press, Cheshire, CT, 1983.
[6] Louis Silverstein, "Graphics at The New York Times," presented at the *First General Conference on Social Graphics*, Leesburg, Virginia, October 23, 1978.

Chapter 13

[1] F. J. Anscombe, "Graphs in Statistical Analysis," *American Statistician,* 27, February 1973; quoted in Edward R. Tufte, *The Visual Display of Quantitative Information,* Graphics Press, Cheshire, CT, 1983.

[2] *Los Angeles Times,* July 22, 1979; based on the work of Gregory J. McRae, California Institute of Technology; quoted in Edward R. Tufte, *The Visual Display of Quantitative Information,* Graphics Press, Cheshire, CT, 1983.

[3] T. J. Mason, F. W. McKay, R. Hoover, W. J. Blot, and J. F. Fraumani Jr., *Atlas of Cancer Mortality for U.S. Counties: 1950-1969,* Washington, DC, Public Health Service, National Institutes of Health, 1975. Maps re-drawn by Lawrence Fahey and Edward Tufte in Edward R. Tufte, *The Visual Display of Quantitative Information,* Graphics Press, Cheshire, CT, 1983.

[4] A. H. Miller, E. N. Goldenburg, and L. Erbring, "Type-Set Politics: Im-pact of Newspapers on Public Confidence," *American Political Science Re-view,* 73, 1979; quoted in Edward R. Tufte, *The Visual Display of Quanti-tative Information,* Graphics Press, Cheshire, CT, 1983.

[5] Darrell Huff, and Irving Geis, *How to Lie with Statistics,* W. W. Norton New York, 1954.

[6] National Science Foundation, *Science Indicators, 1974,* Washington, DC, 1976; quoted in Edward R. Tufte, *The Visual Display of Quantitative Infor-mation,* Graphics Press, Cheshire, CT, 1983. The example cited is drawn from a more detailed analysis presented in Tufte's book.

[7] *New York Times,* August 9, 1978; quoted in Edward R. Tufte, *The Visual Display of Quantitative Information,* Graphics Press, Cheshire, CT, 1983.

[8] *TIME,* April 9, 1979; quoted in Tufte, Edward R., *The Visual Display of Quantitative Information,* Graphics Press, Cheshire, CT, 1983.

[9] D. T. Campbell, and H. L. Ross, "The Connecticut Crackdown on Speed-ing: Time-Series Data in Quasi-Experimental Analysis," in Edward R. Tufte, *The Visual Display of Quantitative Information,* Graphics Press, Cheshire, CT, 1983.

Chapter 16

[1] David Ogilvy, *Ogilvy on Advertising,* Crown Books, New York, 1983.

Chapter 17

[1] K. R. Boff and J. E. Lincoln, *Engineering Data Compendium: Human Per-ception and Performance,* AAMRL, Wright-Patterson Air Force Base, Day-ton, OH, 1988.

[2] T. A. Coonan, R. J. Glushko, and J. E. Weaver, "Hypertext Engineering: Practical Methods for Creating a Compact Disk Encyclopedia," *ACM Con-ference of Document Processing Systems,* Santa Fe, NM, December 1988.

[3] U.S. *Designer's Associate,* contract AF#33615-86-C-0542.

INDEX